D0761031

RAMSES II

This text is an abridged version of research that appeared in
Christiane Desroches Noblecourt's
Ramsès II, La véritable histoire,
(éditions Pygmalion-Gérard Watelet, 1996).

French text abridged by Marie-Delphine Martellière
Translated from the French by David Radzinowicz
Design: Thierry Renard
Copy-editing: Mark Hutchinson
Proofreading: Penny Isaac
Typesetting: Thomas Gravemaker
Color Separation: Dupont, Paris
Maps and drawings: Élisabeth David, Pygmalion

Distributed in North America by Rizzoli International Publications, Inc.

Simultaneously published in French as *Ramsès II*
© Flammarion, Paris, 2007

English-language edition
© Flammarion, 2007

www.editions.flammarion.com

07 08 09 3 2 1

ISBN: 978-2-0803-0043-0

Ouvrage publié avec le concours du Ministère français chargé de la culture–Centre national du livre.

Published with the assistance of the French Ministry of Culture–Centre national du livre.

Dépôt légal: 09/2007

Printed in Italy by Canale

Christiane Desroches Noblecourt

RAMSES II

An Illustrated Biography

Flammarion

Contents

PREFACE   8

1 RAMSES' FIRST STEPS IN THE FLEDGLING DYNASTY   10

There was once a great soldier…
Pa-Ramessu the Vizier
The advent of Ramses I
Prince Seti
Ramses I in the Valley of the Kings
An exceptionally gifted child
The co-regency

The reasons behind the justification
The world of the co-regent
The co-regent at work
The Valley of the Kings
The Valley of the Queens
The co-regent at war
The rise to power

2 CONSECRATION AND THE START OF A LONG REIGN   32

The accession
Time to create a persona
Becoming pharaoh
The purification of the prince
The "suckling"
Ceremonial garb and the placing
   of the crowns
The establishment of the titulary
The transmission of a millennial heritage
The *ished* tree and the longevity of Pharaoh
The great festival of Opet
King and builder
The selection of a new high priest
   of Amun at Karnak
Further constructions

The first acts of Pharaoh's reign
The early years of Ramses' rule
The monuments of Abydos
Work at Pi-Ramesse
A hymn to the Nile
Monuments in Thebes
A well for the miners in the deserts of Kuban
The Kuban Stele
The first Syrian campaign
Preparing the second Syrian campaign
Ramses' army
The four infantry divisions
Supply corps and force composition
Arsenal and bridgeheads
The eve of the second Syrian expedition

3 THE BATTLE OF KADESH   60

Why Kadesh?
The battle of Kadesh as described
   in the "Poem of Pentaur"
The battle of Kadesh as described in
   the military Bulletin
The departure of the army
An enemy trick
Setting up the royal camp

The consequences of the trick
The fray
The Nearin arrive
The Egyptian cavalry charge
The end of the combat
The evening after battle
"Peace is better than combat" (Muwatallis)
The return to Egypt

4   RAMSES, THE BUILDER-KING   86

The immediate consequences of Kadesh
Towards the temples of the south
The tri-unity after
   Amenophis IV-Akhenaten
The return of Seth

The architectural program
The favorite temple: the Ramesseum
Ramses' hidden agenda
The *mammisi* of the king at Thebes
Abu Simbel

5   THE PATH TO PEACE   126

Moab and Edom
Did the Exodus occur under Ramses II?
Foreign manpower under Pharaoh
An indispensable workforce?
The plagues of Egypt?
The views of Egyptologists
The Exodus: an attempt at a reconstitution
The Libyan neighbors
Ramses, quarrymen, and artists
Syria regained
The first seizure of Dapur
The warriors' reward
The counter-offensive of the confederation
Dapur again retaken
The death of Muwatallis

The wellbeing of the country
Revolt in Irem
The choice of royal sons for the war
The diplomacy of Ramses and conflict
   in the Middle East
The Hittites' enforced retreat
New Great Royal Wives
The inauguration of Meha and Ibshek
The message of the temples
The spectacle
Back to earthly realities
The peace negotiations
The peace treaty
Immediate consequences
The crown prince changes his name

6   THE COMING OF THE GOD-KING   160

Death of the queen mother
In the Set-Neferu
The opulence of Egypt
Two sons of Ramses
Change of viceroy in Nubia
The death of the Great Royal Wife Nefertari
Isisnofret appears
A new high priest of Amun
Home affairs: Ramses applies the *maat*
Foreign affairs: the beginning of a friendship
The first jubilee of the thirtieth year
Pharaoh's new lease of life
Meha hit by an earth tremor
Ramses' intrigues
Engagement proposals
Isisnofret and the second jubilee
Ramses goes too far in his demands

Ramses and his capital await the princess
An exceptional marriage
Maathorneferure, Great Royal Wife
The Blessing of Ptah
Those great royal ladies
Ramses and Prince Khaemwaset
The scholars show good sense
From the third to the fourth jubilee
The period of the fourth jubilee
The death of Hattusilis
The sixth jubilee
The seventh jubilee
The eighth jubilee
The ninth jubilee
The tenth jubilee
The eleventh jubilee
The twelfth, thirteenth, and fourteenth jubilees

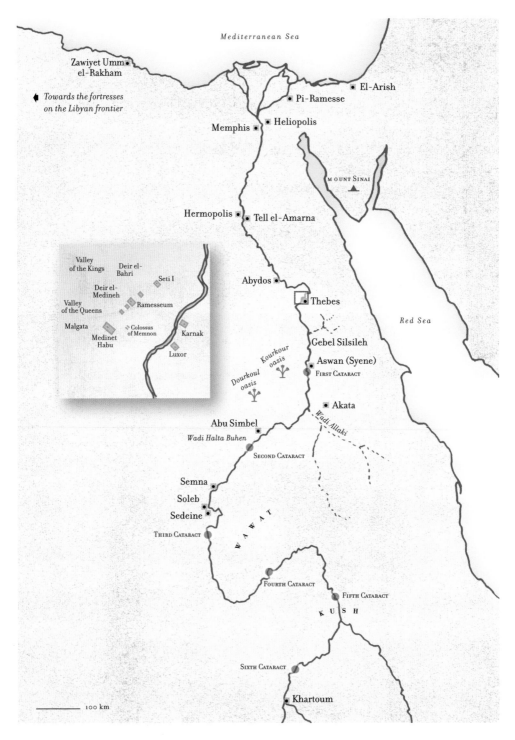

The Nile Valley at the junction of the White Nile and Blue Nile.

7 THE LAST MIRACLE OF RAMSES

222

New Year's Day, July 1213 BCE
Pharaoh's farewell
The funerary banquet

The tomb plundered
A royal hiding-place

CONCLUSION

240

So lived Usermaatre-Setepenre,
  Ramses Meryamun
2,830 years later
Ramses in Cairo
Ramses in need of care

Ramses in Paris
Pharaoh and his 110 carers
An unexpected and important revelation
The problem affecting the mummy
To cure a king

INDEX

250

BIBLIOGRAPHY

252

Preface

Within the borders of his native land and beyond, the name of Ramses the Great has remained over the centuries that of an undisputed hero. But what is his true place among the Pharaohs of the marvelous land of Egypt?

In fact, in the period of its history known as the New Kingdom (Nineteenth and Twentieth Dynasties), ancient Egypt boasts several sovereigns with the birth name Ramses, but the one of whom popular history is most fond is the son of King Seti I Men-Maat-Re and of the noble lady Tuya.

According to information set down by Ramses himself (see the "400 year stele" in the Cairo Museum), the king hailed from a family of senior officials from the eastern Nile delta, on the fringes of the Semitic world. At the time the young prince Ramses ascended to his father's throne, the memory of the great deeds of the high-ranking dignitaries who had ruled Egypt in the previous period of the Middle Kingdom, the Amenemhet and Sesostris dynasty that had defended its southern borders, was still vivid.

In his role as defender of his country, Ramses had been given the first name of User-Maat-Re ("The justice of Re [the vital force of the Sun] is powerful"). The southern frontier at that time had been secured; the danger for the country came from the northeast, where the Indo-European Hittites*—seconded by a confederation of eastern Mediterranean coastal tribes—threatened to invade the Nile delta. To keep them at bay, by the fifth year of his reign Ramses had contrived to break up the coalition the Hittites had built up with their Middle Eastern allies and had halted their advance in Syria, at the famous battle of Kadesh on the Orontes. The result was the earliest known peace treaty in antiquity, paving the way for a fruitful period during which Ramses consolidated Egypt's peaceful relations with her eastern neighbors. In conformity, moreover, with the efforts of his royal predecessors, Thutmosis and Amenophis, Ramses further reinforced the prospect for peace by adding to the treaty a concluding

Hittites: Indo-European people who invaded Asia Minor and subjected the indigenous people, the Hattis, in the 27th cent. BCE.

clause concerning his union with the daughter of his one-time adversary, the valiant chief of the Hittites. The princess married the Egyptian sovereign as soon as she arrived in his homeland and was promptly "baptized", in the local style, Maat-Hor-Neferu-Re ("She who sees Horus,* the creative power of the Sun").

With his many wives and innumerable children, the reputation the king enjoyed as a "miracle-worker" was encouraged by the monarch himself, and it is this image that endures to this day. Indeed, so powerful is the "aura" surrounding this magnificent sovereign that his mummy was even transferred to the Centre d'Energie Nucléaire in Saclay, in France, in a bid to save it by radiation treatment from the threat of deterioration. The analyses involved in these conservation efforts revealed, among other things, that Ramses the Great was riddled with arteriosclerosis and that his hair had a coppery-red tinge that underlined the Near-Eastern origins of this son of Seti.

Throughout his entire reign, by means of gigantic monuments and countless texts, he did his utmost to ensure that the glorious story of his rule would echo down the ages.

Christiane Desroches Noblecourt

Horus: lord of heaven, a major divinity in the Egyptian pantheon, Horus fulfills various functions. He can appear either as a falcon or as a man with a falcon's head.

RAMSES' FIRST STEPS IN THE FLEDGLING DYNASTY

There was once a great soldier . . .

I T WAS PHARAOH HOREMHEB (1327–1295 BCE), a soldier and an administrator at heart, who restored order and security to crippled Egypt. His famous edict against corrupt officials underscores the extent to which sloppiness had infected the country, as well as serious negligence, corruption, and contempt for the law. Under the strong leadership of her worthy master, however, Egypt regained esteem and respect abroad.

Horemheb's entourage and collaborators had been selected with considerable acumen, and the king had presumably noticed the most brilliant among them, a young soldier of the name of Pa-Ramessu, who very quickly rose to the rank of troop commander. He was the son of a certain Seti who came from the eastern borders of the delta, one of the strongholds of the god Seth on the site of the town of Avaris, which became the capital of the Hyksos invaders. The place is

Horemheb, last king of Egypt of the Eighteenth Dynasty, reigned 1333–1306 BCE.

located on the "Waters of Re" (the easternmost Nilotic branch of the delta), in the direction of the citadel of Tjaru (Sila). It lies on the "Ways of Horus," the starting point of the coastal road that crossed the country of Canaan, where Seth was recognized as the Asiatic Baal. Placing this son under the tutelage of Seth was probably designed not only to signal his local roots, but also to bring out other family links.

Pa-Ramessu was in all likelihood slightly younger than his sovereign. He climbed the ladder of a military career beside his pharaoh, whose first concern had been to make the army strong enough to defend Egypt's interests beyond its frontiers. Exceeding the functions formerly carried out by his father, he rose to be Master of the Royal Horse. As was natural, he was then promoted to the crack chariot corps. Once he had become a chariot driver, Horemheb entrusted him with a still more enviable post: Royal Envoy to Foreign Lands, with the responsibility for transmitting diplomatic missives. He was then named general, and sent by Pharaoh to command the fortress at Tjaru, a border post through which all the military expeditions to the east would pass. In addition to this, as the newly appointed Controller of the Mouth of the Nile, he now had the duty of ensuring the safety of the north of the country to both east and west.

Gold signet-ring of Pharaoh Horemheb. Egyptian Art, New Kingdom, Nineteenth Dynasty. Musée du Louvre, Paris.

Seth: bellicose god and "troublemaker," Seth is however also the guardian of royalty and the overseer of infertile land.

Pa-Ramessu the Vizier

THE FACT THAT PA-RAMESSU juggled all these responsibilities so confidently prompted Horemheb to elevate him to the post of vizier, adding the title of Deputy of the King in Upper and Lower Egypt, in which capacity he probably supervised the works on the Temple of Karnak.

Horemheb, to placate the higher clergy of Amun,* had had the great temple and all the chapels in honor of the disk of Aten, which had been erected in the east of Karnak by Amenophis IV at the beginning of his reign, taken down. On orders, it would seem, from Pa-Ramessu, most of the elements of which they were composed were subsequently concealed inside the Ninth Pylon. By royal permission, Pa-Ramessu was also given the honor of appearing at the foot of the eastern tower of the pylon,* in the form of two statues in which he is represented squatting and clad in a vast robe with the collar of the vizier, all "gifts from His Majesty". Finally, with the investiture of Pa-Ramessu as crown prince over the whole country, the die was definitively cast; he had, in effect, been appointed as the successor to Horemheb, who had no heir of

Amun: one of the principal divinities of the Egyptian pantheon. He can appear as Min, god of fertility, and at Karnak is also venerated in the aspect of Amun-Re. Divinity of the Theban region.

Pylon: monumental entrance to a temple formed of two solid masses of masonry of trapezoidal form framing a doorway.

*Pa-Ramessu, the future
Ramses I, in his vizier's
robes. Egyptian sculpture,
New Kingdom,
Eighteenth Dynasty,
Egyptian Museum, Cairo.*

his own. Pa-Ramessu, on the other hand, was lucky enough to possess a son, the active Seti, who may have been appointed second vizier at this time. The investiture was celebrated in great style. The seal-ring bearing the title was received in the presence of senior officials; singing and dancing accompanied the incumbent to his residence, where the festivities continued in the family home.

His wife was the lady Sitre. His son, Seti, was most probably already married to the young Tuya, daughter of Raia, a chariot lieutenant, and a member of the chorus of Amun, Ruia. The young couple already had a little girl, Tia, and perhaps also a son, thought to have died in adolescence. At all events, another son came into the world, whom his parents named after his grandfather, according to custom: Ramses. It was surely from this time that Pa-Ramessu had himself called Ramessu, deleting from his name the demonstrative article "Pa," which now seemed beneath him.

The advent of Ramses I

WHEN THE PHARAOH HOREMHEB died, in 1295, Ramses, son of Seti and Tuya, would have been in his fifth year. He will certainly have attended the crowning of his grandfather, the first

Ramses Menpehtyre. It was this last who became the founding ancestor of the new dynasty, that of the Ramessides, the Nineteenth.

To ensure closer links with the preceding line of pharaohs, Ramses I chose for the site where his hypogeum* was to be dug in the royal necropolis beneath the Theban Mountain, the "Great Field" (Ta-sekhet-aat, the Valley of the Kings) to the west of Thebes. He assumed that the craftsmen of the guild of the "Place of Truth" (the Set-Maat, at Deir el-Medineh) created by Amenophis I would have time to provide a deep rock-cut tomb to receive his royal remains. In addition, he introduced innovations: as the founder, with Sitre, of a dynasty, he also wanted his queen to benefit from a vault in a necropolis destined to house the queens of the new line.

It may have been Prince Seti who was charged with finding the most suitable site. His choice alighted on a wadi* that opens broadly onto the western plain of Thebes in the south of the Valley of the Kings, the Set-Neferu or Valley of the Queens. The necropolis had already been employed for burials of senior officials, as well as for royal offspring of the preceding dynasty. The mountainous site was dominated by the Holy Cave dedicated to the great feminine principle of Hathor, in the depths of which the dead were inhumed.

The new pharaoh then undertook a project he had long cherished: to continue the architectural plans of Amenophis III at Karnak and thereby, in the eyes of the priests of Amun who had been frustrated

Hypogeum:
in general,
a rock-cut tomb.

Wadi: watercourse,
generally dry, but which
can suddenly fill up with
a great quantity of water.

*The four papyrus columns
in the botanical gardens of
the Akhmenu (festival
hall, exceptionally in
stone) of Thutmosis III.
Temple of Amun-Re.
Karnak, Upper Egypt.*

and mistreated during the Amarnian period, celebrate the return to their cult. By the end of the reign of Horemheb, the center of the great courtyard in front of the Pylon of Amenophis (the Third Pylon) was set with an avenue of twelve very tall columns. He also completed the colonnade and began to flank it with a series of less elevated structures with closed-papyrus capitals; work started with the north wing. His plan, which would be carried on by his son Seti and his grandson Ramses II, was to erect a very large hall evoking an immense forest of papyrus; it is still visible today in the vast temple at Karnak. The decoration had not yet been done, but on walls once decorated by the order of Horemheb he now had the name (*nomen*) and first name (*prenomen*) of his former master replaced with his own.

Prince Seti

A T THAT TIME, MEMPHIS was the military capital whence General, now Pharaoh Horemheb restored order to the once tottering organization. Seti was clearly of great assistance to his father, who was now exhausted by a long and busy career. In reality, he acted as co-regent and was not above proclaiming: "While he was Re, the Sun radiant at dawn, I was by his side like a star of the earth." He was also desirous of showing his authority in regions formerly under the suzerainty of Egypt, whose denizens, the Kharu, Djahy, and Fenkhu, had proved less than loyal to the home country and had thereby weakened her position. It was also necessary to ensure that taxes were regularly collected, because every New Year the mayors of the subjugated foreign towns, just like their counterparts in Egyptian cities, had to pay taxes to the crown—and, in particular, to the great temple of Amun—as well as contribute to building work there.

As Ramses the Great, eager to emphasize his extraordinary precocity at every turn, was later to point up, it was no surprise that Prince Seti should have had his young son, who was seven years old at the time, take part in this incursion into the Asian lands flanking the Mediterranean coast as far as southern Phoenicia (Fenkhu). The few prisoners taken in Canaan, always accompanied by women and children, were then employed to supplement the personnel of the temple at Buhen (in Lower Egyptian Nubia). The expedition was led by Seti, who was to erect two steles commemorating the event, while Ramses I, now in the second year of his reign, resided at Memphis, closely supervising the foundation of his new capital, Pi-Ramesse (the "Domain of Ramses").

Ramses I in the Valley of the Kings

SHORTLY AFTER CONFIRMING the title of co-regent on his son, Ramses died: his reign had lasted scarcely two years, though he had already effectively shared the burden of power for many years with Horemheb. Ramses I was buried in the heart of the Valley of the Kings, in a tomb that remained unfinished but in which extracts from a new compilation of royal funerary texts, the *Book of Gates*, appeared. On a bluish-gray ground, the sober elegance of the vibrantly colored décor remains visible. His wife Sitre soon followed him to the land of Osiris:* her little vault in the Valley of the Queens was hastily adorned with black-line figures retouched in red. The Ramessid era was born.

Osiris: god of the dead who oversees the survival of the deceased in the afterworld. His symbol is the *djed* pillar and his attributes include the scepter (crook) and flail, which he holds across the chest.

An exceptionally gifted child

IT IS SOMETIMES HARD to reconstruct and understand the true history of an event when the ancient evidence is strongly marked by rhetoric and myth. Today, the expressions used by Ramses are often judged as presenting symptoms of ponderous self-aggrandizement, of megalomania even. It would be easy to fall in with this condemnation were one to ignore two crucial factors. The first requires us to think back to the time in which the events occurred and to take into account the florid language of Egypt's inhabitants generally. The second is more specifically political, and pertains closely to Ramses the man and to the carefully calculated plan that he made his life's work: to create and impose an image of himself as an exceptional being, an extraordinary figure born to carry all before him. He reveals himself as domineering but munificent, always taking inspiration from the divine, since he is of its very essence: though a *parvenu*, a redhead, scorned apparently by Horus, born of the line of Seth, he is the son of the sun on earth and dear to Amun—in short, he is a worker of miracles.

It was hard, then, not to further embroider what was already an exceptionally gifted childhood, during which he was ably to assist his royal father while still very young. In was in this spirit that the famous dedicatory inscription of Abydos, an obligatory point of reference in this connection, was conceived and carved by Ramses' order at the very gates to the temple founded by Seti. At the site of the largest and most popular of all holy shrines, Ramses leapt at the opportunity to ensure his posterity.

If we take the text literally, it would seem that the young prodigy was hardly out of the nursery when his father raised him up to sit by

Pages 18–19:
Interior of the tomb of Ramses I: detail of a mural with the snake, Mehen, and the twelve goddesses, symbols of the twelve hours of the night, which he has to devour. Valley of the Kings, Thebes-West.

his side on the throne. Reading the account, hugely important for the history of the co-regency and for Ramses himself, it appears more probable that it was Seti who was intent on stressing the might of his fledgling dynasty by emphasizing the qualities and education of the crown prince. The reported events certainly took place, but Ramses must have been rather older.

No doubt the genuine precocity of his son would have encouraged Seti to entrust him with certain official responsibilities so that no one could ever dispute his right to the crown. In all probability, Seti took his inspiration from Horemheb's intentions for Pa-Ramessu when he made his designated successor "Crown Prince to the Whole Land."

The co-regency

THE ELEVATION, THEN, probably occurred during the period of peace that followed the agreement concluded by Seti I with the Hittite prince Muwatallis—in all likelihood, between the seventh and eighth years of Seti's reign, by which time Prince Ramses would have entered his fifteenth year. Before all the great and the good of the kingdom, and representatives from the assembled people, and probably in the vast court of the temple at Memphis, the sovereign presented his son for nomination as king by his right hand.

As Ramses was to write: "I issue from Re ... while I was raised by my father Men-maat-re (Seti I). The Universal Lord himself magnified me when I was a child until I became ruler. He made me the land whilst I was in the egg, the great ones were smelling the earth [prostrating themselves] before me when I was inducted as elder son to be Hereditary Prince upon the throne of Geb."

The reasons behind the justification

CERTAIN IMPROBABILITIES in the account give the lie to Ramses' insistence on presenting the event as sanctioning his position as crown prince right from the start—something which, to my eyes, seems excessive if the subject had been truly beyond all doubt. Ramses presents himself as incredibly precocious, but insists, too, on the fact that he was "inducted as elder son and Hereditary Prince upon the throne of Geb," as if he wanted to show that he had received these prerogatives, instead of their being allotted to him from the outset. Ramses' repeated justifications of his legitimacy persisted even up to the third year of his reign, when on the stele of Kuban he stated to his courtiers: "While you were still in the egg, you already formed projects in your capacity as crown prince. You were kept informed of the problems faced by the Two Lands while you were still very young, still sporting the side-lock of youth. You stood at the head of the army when only a ten-year-old stripling."

At one time the great American Egyptologist in Chicago, James Henry Breasted, advanced a hypothesis, based on a relief on the outer wall of the hypostyle at Karnak on which, behind Seti's chariot, the outline of a little prince can be seen, hammered out and replaced by that of the young Ramses. This substitution, he argued, was proof that Ramses had assassinated an elder brother and usurped his place. This hypothesis does not stand up if one looks back to the scene of the Jubilee Temple of Seti at Gurna, where the picture showing Ramses crowned by Amon in the presence of Seti I proves there was perfect harmony between father and son. Such justifications were perhaps aimed at grooming for the throne a candidate from outside the family of the Ramses, a forgotten descendant of the last kings of the Eighteenth Dynasty. At all events, the fact that the figure was obliterated after featuring on a wall at Karnak shows the final victory of the Ramessides. If the corrections verge on the improbable, it nonetheless appears that it was on this occasion that the young man "received the crowns" and his "throne name." Henceforth, whenever texts refer to the prince co-regent, the throne name all invested sovereigns are granted at that point is also added.

The world of the co-regent

THE PALACE OF THE CO-REGENT was most probably built in the city of Memphis. Charming noble ladies would have attended Ramses' first two Great Royal Wives, but information on their origin is scanty at best. It is known that one queen was called Nefertari, and the other, Isisnofret. The first, whose charm and beauty were vaunted by Ramses, must have been of fragile health: chief queen, she seems to have vanished from the kingdom around the twenty-fourth or twenty-fifth years of the reign. The second, Isisnofret, on the other hand, survived beyond the fortieth year.

Very quickly, both women gave Ramses their first child. Nefertari gave birth to a first son immediately, Imenherwenemef ("Amun is on his right hand"), while Isisnofret produced a little girl, Bentanat ("Daughter of the goddess Anat"). The question

Pharaoh Seti I as Osiris. Temple of Seti I, Abydos.

immediately arises: why was Isisnofret's child placed under the protection of an Asian goddess? Was Isisnofret a Syrian princess, raised in the royal harem? There is no evidence for this. Note should be taken, however, of the extent to which the worship of Asiatic divinities had penetrated local practices, to say nothing of Egypt's military sorties into Canaan and Amurru. More generally, numerous foreigners, established for several generations in the country, now had careers there, for the people of the country of the Nile (and the point bears repeating), if they were always deeply patriotic, were no xenophobes. Ramses himself, not only in his adolescence but in later life as well, was surrounded by Egyptian senior officials seconded by luminaries from abroad.

Let us cite, by way of example, Paser, son of High Priest Nebneteru, the youthful chamberlain of Seti appointed Head of the Secrets of the Two Ladies (Keeper of the Royal Crowns), who probably placed the *pschent* (double crown) on the head of the royal heir, accompanied at the time by a childhood friend, Imenemipet. On the other hand, Ashahebsed, who in the eighth year of Seti's reign inscribed the hymns to his two masters on the mountains of the Sinai, was probably not of Egyptian origin—a fact that did nothing to

Tomb of Nefertari: the queen on her knees in adoration, Valley of the Queens. (Taken from Nina Davis, Ancient Egyptian Paintings, *Chicago, 1936; library of the Musée du Louvre.)*

Bentanat, Great Royal Wife, at the feet of the colossus of Ramses II, Temple of Karnak.

prevent him rising to the lofty position of Royal Envoy to All Foreign Lands. Similarly, General Urhiya, who was born in northern Syria, gave his son the Canaanite name of Yupa. One of the first to establish himself in the service of the pharaoh was the Head of the Painters of the Temple at Karnak, Didia, whose ancestor Pedubaal had come from Canaan to Egypt six generations previously.

The co-regent at work

DURING THE EIGHTH year of Seti's reign, Ramses the co-regent wasted no time getting to grips with the dispatches sent to his father by Imenemipet, viceroy of Nubia, concerning a revolt brewing in the land of Kush (modern Sudan). Seti outlined a strategy, and, in seven days, the rebellion was quashed by infantry accompanied by a detachment of chariots. By the end, Ramses would see close to a thousand prisoners brought to Thebes, together with much African plunder.

Throughout the ninth year of his reign, Pharaoh Seti made a point of personally supervising the construction of his temple at Abydos. The prince co-regent, meanwhile, was responsible for monitoring the rest of his vast architectural programme: the Palace of Pi-Ramesse to the east of the delta, the shrines he wanted to see throughout Egypt, and the great monuments of Thebes. On the right bank at Karnak, in the huge royal domain dedicated to Amun, the great hypostyle hall* was under construction, while on the left bank there was his Temple of a Million Years in Gurna. In the company of Paser, recently promoted to southern vizier, Ramses paid special attention to the great rock-cut tomb being prepared for Seti.

Architectural planning went hand in hand with the garnering of the materials required to embellish them, such as granite from Aswan and gold from Nubia. In the course of his inspections between the ninth and tenth year, the prince regent would have seized the opportunity to get to know the guilds of highly skilled Theban craftsmen and to discover their work. Their efforts were in general anonymous, a state of affairs that would change slightly during the Ramesside period. Names appeared, chiefly revealed in excavations at the village of the craftsmen of the royal tombs at Thebes, Set-Maat (modern Deir el-Medina).

Hypostyle hall: enclosed space with a ceiling borne on columns.

Facing page: The portico with rectangular pillars showing scenes of the cult of Seti I. Temple of Seti I, Abydos.

The Valley of the Kings

UNDER THE DIRECTION of Sennedjem, and following plans quite different from those for previous royal tombs, the craftsmen worked on the sepultures of Seti I and Tuya. For Seti, an immense shaft almost a hundred meters in length was bored into the limestone rock of the Valley of the Kings. In a décor primarily given over to the sovereigns, the contents of the funerary books would evoke the phases of the sun as it recharged its energy during the night, while genii filed through mysterious paths that wound towards rebirth.

The Valley of the Queens

R AMSES ALSO TOOK PAINS to visit the Valley of the Queens farther to the south, where the Chief Royal Wife of the dynasty—his paternal grandmother—had been inhumed. There he was to inspect the early stages of the digging of a tomb destined for his much-venerated mother, Tuya. The plan for the sepulture, which was on two levels and highly geometrical, harmoniously incorporated two successive flights of stairs leading down to a pair of main rooms underground. The second of these, which was huge and had four pillars reserved in the rock, was to receive the sovereign's body. The plans

Bust of Merytamun, daughter of Ramses II. Ramesseum, Thebes.

for the highly varied religious décor, like the texts, were drawn from *The Book of the Dead*.

Back in Memphis after his long sojourn in the south, the crowned prince found his family flourishing. Isisnofret, already mother of Bentanat and a little Ramses, had just given birth to another particularly vigorous boy, who was named Khaemwaset ("who appears at Thebes"). Though still so young, one of the daughters Nefertari had recently produced, Merytamun, was already blessed with all the beauty and elegance of her mother. Ramses had just turned twenty and was still under the spell of his stay in Upper Egypt with Paser, in the company of foremen at the great temples and Theban decorators. Seti, meanwhile, forged ahead with his program: not content with advancing the plans for the largest hypostyle hall in Egypt, in the eleventh year of his reign he ordered the building of a second one at the Temple of Gebel Barkal*, the sanctuary of Amun of Napata, in the kingdom of Kush (modern Sudan).

Ramses did not neglect the region of the Waters of Re, the eastern branch of the Nile delta, where Seti had enlarged his father's small palace. From the finest workshops in Memphis, the co-regents commissioned glazed tiles and flagstones in various colors (the predominant hue being turquoise) to decorate the doors and windows of the palace, the floor of the royal platform, and the entrance ramps.

The co-regent at war

I N THE LIGHT OF REPORTS from messengers that hinted at minor disturbances in the offing to the south as well as to the east, the apparently secure peace between Egypt and her external possessions began to waver. Doubtless Seti would have put his twenty-two-year-old son in command of a small expedition designed to forestall events in Canaan and in the outlying lands haunted by the Bedouin Shasus. It is, at all events, beyond question that he entrusted him, in the thirteenth and fourteenth years of Seti's reign, with officially receiving in the pharaoh's place tributes from the lands of Wawat, and more especially from Kush (Lower and Upper Nubia).

The role of the youthful co-regent was now so pivotal that he was given permission to commemorate his personal promotion on the walls of a *hemispeos** dug into a cliff in Nubia at Beit el-Wali. On the walls, Ramses appears as a pharaoh in his own right. The north wall in the open-air court is carved with reliefs summarizing the Asian and Libyan campaigns. Ramses appears in all the ardor of youth, astride the box of his chariot and about to overturn an enemy already

Shabti *of prince Khaemwaset, son of Ramses II. Egyptian Sculpture, Paris, Musée du Louvre.*

Gebel Barkal: rocky headland overlooking the site of Napata. Also called the "pure mountain," it was regarded as the residence of the god Amun.

Hemispeos: temple whose main mass is dug out of a cliff, but possessed of a fore-section like a courtyard in front.

terrorized by the co-regent's battle lion. In the distance, an Asian citadel is attacked. A spectacle still richer in vivid details is the long, carved and at one time polychrome register presenting the military action in Upper Nubia: an attack from a tribe of African type is repulsed by pharaoh's forces, led by Ramses standing on his chariot; for the first time, he is accompanied by two of his sons: Imenherwenemef and Khaemwaset, each in his own chariot. At full tilt, the charge completely routs the rebels. Then follows the interminable procession of tributes carried or led by the subdued vassals: various African animals—lions, giraffes, cheetahs, gazelles, long-tailed monkeys—and the produce that adorned Egyptian life: elephant tusks, ostrich feathers, ebony, locally manufactured furniture in the purest Egyptian style, animal skins, spices, all kinds of semiprecious stones, and, finally, small bags of gold, gold rings, and even decorative gold jewelry of consummate craftsmanship.

Did this Nubian campaign actually take place at this time or should the scene be viewed as recalling the punitive expedition in the eighth year of Seti's reign to the land of Irem (Kush)? The Sudanese appearance of the fleeing inhabitants seems to militate in favor of this hypothesis. The eighth year being the time of Ramses' marriage, the prince could obviously not allude to any putative offspring; at the time the picture was composed, however, he seems to have conflated two periods—the eighth year of Seti's reign, when the events would have occurred, and the thirteenth and fourteenth years, when the little princes were aged five and four respectively. Similarly, the events

Ramses, assisted by the two princes, pursues the rebels of Upper Nubia.

recorded on the northern wall may allude to the Asiatic and Libyan expeditions on which Ramses had accompanied his father.

The rise to power

SUCH IS THE HISTORICAL lesson of the first of the seven main sanctuaries founded by Ramses in Nubia. Above all, it would seem to constitute a proclamation of his imminent seizure of personal power at the very moment Seti I was on the wane, in all probability due to illness. The rear of the *speos*, dug out primitively in the sandstone, presents Ramses alone paying homage to the divine forms and ultimately presenting the regal and supreme offering of *maat**—that is, the balance and dynamism inherent in all things, which is a constant concern for pharaoh, who must ensure its presence and effectiveness.

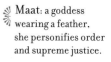 Maat: a goddess wearing a feather, she personifies order and supreme justice.

Kheperesh: blue "war crown".

So that none may be unaware of his divine essence, he is shown in the sanctum sanctorum twice as a child-king, but wearing the *kheperesh** of the kingdom, suckled by Isis and by Anuket who reigns over the cataracts of the Nile. With such forebears, and after such exploits, how could anyone doubt his worthiness to assume the Two Crowns? Between the fourteenth and fifteenth years of his reign, Seti I, who might have been supposed to be in the prime of life, died, unexpectedly it would seem, approaching his fiftieth year. Ramses had just turned twenty-five.

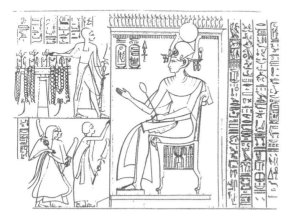

Imenherwenemef, eldest son of Ramses, the vizier, and Viceroy Imenemipet, present tributes to Ramses as co-regent.

2

CONSECRATION AND THE START OF A LONG REIGN

The accession

S ETI I HAD PASSED AWAY. His son and co-regent, Ramses, now had to affirm himself as a worthy heir to a family of valiant soldiers rigorously trained to arms and to palace discipline. The man who had occupied the post of co-regent from his youth was now confronted with the last stage in the absolute possession of the throne: to undergo the trials of consecration and fathom the mysteries of the supreme investiture.

Shortly after the death of his father, at dawn on the twenty-seventh day of the third month of summer (*shemu*), his accession was speedily proclaimed. He now had to await the seventy days of preparation before the imposing Ceremony of Burial, which was to take place in the Valley of the Kings at the beginning of the second month of the Flood.

The vizier Paser, who attended the consecration and placed the double crown (pschent) on his master's head.

Time to create a persona

IN MEMPHIS AND HELIOPOLIS, everything was ready for Ramses, who, having already been established on the throne, was preparing himself for the impressive initiation during which he would take full possession of the Two Crowns. The coronation ceremonies would mark the true onset of the reign. During the vigil which preceded the reappearance of the moon and the dawn of the crowning, Ramses pondered his destiny. Admittedly, he was the son of a king; but he sensed the imperative need, once the festivities were over, to devote a lengthy text to affirming with great solemnity his indisputable right to assume the throne of Horus. Perhaps this was an attempt to finesse the dubious circumstances of his accession to the co-regency, to erase his military family origins and his close links with the world of Seti, or even the ties of some of his ancestors (such as his great-uncle, who had married the sister of a friend of the young Tutankhamun) to the circle of the Amarna* reformers? In truth, since the reign of Horemheb, the new masters of the country had evinced no real animosity to the Amarna period, so in the *hemispeos* at Beit el-Wali co-regent Ramses was able to employ the process of "sunken relief," an innovation dear to Amarna sculptors.

Amarna, Amarnian: concerning the Tell el-Amarna, the capital of Egypt during the reign of Akhenaten (1353–1337 BCE). By extension the adjective designates the period in general.

Becoming pharaoh

STILL, IT WAS AS WELL to be wary of the world represented by the Amun stronghold of Karnak and to be vigilant in maintaining the balance between real power and the importance of cults dedicated to other aspects of the divine.

In creating his persona, Ramses planned to use the most daring means to force through necessary reforms, adapted to the alien world on the horizon, so that his country might evolve. Everything now depended on how credible he could make his image in the eyes of subjects ever receptive to the charisma of a beneficent lord. He would have, then, to forge a legend and to exceed by means of miraculous deeds the prestige earned by his predecessors. He soon set to work.

The auspices, moreover, seemed propitious. The Sothic period* which occurred every 1,460 years had begun in the year 1313 BCE and had already allowed Seti I to exploit the idea of the "Repeater of Births" that would herald a new era and so bolster his power. Ramses envisaged making the most of this opportunity in a

Sothic period: every 1,460 years, the Egyptians saw the first day of their calendar year coincide with the heliacal rising of Sirius (Sothis). This cycle is known as the "Sothic period."

still more concrete manner, for only thirty-four years separated the year 1313, when the two calendars had coincided, and the date of his crowning, 1279. As the civil calendar lost a day every four years, the two systems, at the time of the coronation, would differ by only a few days, a week at most; our pharaoh, therefore, could still claim to be the sovereign during whose reign Egypt would benefit from this exceptional phenomenon.

Moreover, during a brief naval battle that took place shortly before the death of his father, he had already driven back the Sherden, allies of the Libyans, those "warriors of the sea" who had tried to invade the delta. He had taken prisoners, who had been handed over to his officers and quickly transformed—*mirabile dictu!*—into first-rate mercenaries loyal to their new masters. The program Ramses was tracing for the future must have made him look forward eagerly to the impressive days that lay ahead, since, once initiated and instructed in the secret laws governing the universe, "the heavens would shake, the ground tremble, as he took possession of the kingdom of Re." The initiation ceremony will certainly have been repeated at the rites known as "Confirmation of the Royal Power," celebrated every year on New Year's Day in the Temples of a Million Years of the Kings, at least from the beginning of the New Kingdom, and most probably well before. Luckily, a papyrus mentioning this ritual is preserved in the Brooklyn Museum in New York.

The purification of the prince

A s Ramses awoke at first light, ceremonial priests entered the palace and bore him in a sedan-chair to the gates to the temple pylon, where the ritual of the "Baptism of Pharaoh," which comprised the preliminary phase of the rite was to be performed. These ceremonies had to be performed in the presence of high-ranking officials, though it seems that the queen was not present. Four priests, one bearing the mask of the falcon Horus, a second that of the ibis of Thoth,* a third that of Seth (an as yet unidentified animal reminiscent of an aardvark or, occasionally, an ass), and the last a mask personifying Dun-auy ("the one with outspread wings"), flanked the king to south and north and to east and west. From a golden ewer they poured the sacred libation—portrayed by dashes formed of *ankh* and *was* signs— over Ramses' head and shoulders. Thus purified by this holy aspersion emanating from all four cardinal points, Ramses

Thoth: patron god of scribes. Two animals are dedicated to him: the baboon and the ibis. He can, and this is the most frequent case, take on the aspect of a man with the head of an ibis. Divinity of the Hermopolis region.

Statue of the god Horus lifting his arms to pour water from the purification bowl (since vanished). Egyptian Sculpture, Musée du Louvre, Paris.

would be anointed no fewer than nine times with sacred oils as protection against attacks from the evil one. These ointments came from the venerable sanctuaries of Upper and Lower Egypt and likewise extended Isis's magical protection over Pharaoh's flesh and blood.

The "suckling"

A SECOND PHASE OF THE RITES was about to begin, reflected in the breast-feeding scene sometimes represented on temple walls, in which Pharaoh, intentionally depicted as small but still clothed as a sovereign, is nursed by a divine female image. The scene, which was acted out, was meant to confirm the very essence of Ramses, nourished in the bosom of the cosmos and partaking

thereby of the "water of life." Consequently, all trace of human origin was expunged from the royal image.

Ceremonial garb and the placing of the crowns

IN THE HOLY OF HOLIES, the master of ceremonies conducting the royal personage now gathered up a long red linen stole bearing pictures drawn in ink of thirty white and thirty red crowns, a décor completed by the form of Ptah,* Master of Memphis and of the Royal Jubilees. The fringes of the stole had to be tied sixty times and then placed around Ramses' neck. Next, two scepters—the *ankh* and the *was*—were placed in the king's hands. Ramses was then given two more frontal ornaments—the *seshed* diadem, to which was affixed the *uraeus*, the *shesep* head-band, and the heavy counterweight, the *meankh*, "that which gives divine life." Numerous amulets were then affixed to the red linen stole. Spotless sandals of white skin were then bestowed on Ramses, together with the "Baton of the Foreign Lands" which, at the time of the ritual processions, was to assert dominion over the forces of opposition.

The officiants then proceeded to dress Pharaoh. For an act so rich in symbolism, cladding Ramses in one of those splendid tunics in folded linen that had appeared with profusion in princely wardrobes from the very start of the reigns of Tuthmosis IV and then Amenophis III would have been out of place. The attire of the earliest times seemed *de rigueur*, and Ramses, bare-chested, was to sport just a loincloth, modelled on that of Narmer, the first pharaoh of the historical era.

Then, seated on an archaic-style seat placed on a dais, Ramses, flanked once again by Horus and Thoth (or Seth)—roles always played by the priests who brought him the white crown of the south and the red crown

Facing page:
Bust of a granite statue of Ramses II. British Museum, London.

Ptah: guardian god of artists. He also maintains special links with royalty and plays a significant role in the celebration of the jubilee rites. Divinity of the city of Memphis.

Below left: *The* uraeus—*a female cobra erect with extended hood—is featured on the king's forehead and on the gods' headwear. The snake's magic power is thus placed in the service of Pharaoh. Musée du Louvre, Paris.*

Below center: Ankh, *symbol of life. Tomb of Amenophis II, Valley of the Kings, Thebes-West. Egyptian Museum, Cairo.*

Below right: Was, *symbol of power. Meir. Egyptian Museum, Cairo.*

of the north—now received the double *pschent* comprised of the union of the Two Crowns. The two primal goddesses (or mothers), Nekhebet (often represented by a vulture) and Wadjet (the sacred female cobra), are evoked by two priestesses seated beside Ramses, on whose head they gently balance the *pschent*.

Gesturing rhythmically with the arms to invoke the distant ancestors of the king, the priests, sporting capped hoods with falcons' and dogs' heads personifying the geniuses of the towns of Pe and Nekhen, proceed to receive the monarch. Then, in the chapel made to resemble the primitive sanctuary of Nekhebet, the *Per-ur* ("Great House"), and in that of Wadjet and the north, the *Per-neser* ("House of Flame") or *Per-nu*, various liturgical headdresses are

Detail of a colossal statue of Ramses II: loincloth with a dagger slipped under a belt whose loop features a cartouche carved with the royal name: "Ramses, beloved of Amun." Courtyard of Ramses II, Luxor.

Crowning of Ramses II, protected by the Two Guardian Mothers. The pschent *is here conferred by Horus and Thoth. Karnak.*

presented to the royal recipient and placed, each one in turn, upon his head. These include the *atef* crown of Re, flanked with ostrich feathers, the *seshed* headband, the *hennu* crown, the *ibes* crown-wig, and linen wig-covers, such as the *nemes*.

Finally, after bowing to the master of Karnak, Amun places the ostrich-skin *keperesh* (improperly monikered the "helmet of war" or "war crown") on the head of the new initiate; the *keperesh* will subsequently be worn daily by Pharaoh, testifying to the "function of Atum"* thereby conferred on him to exercise royal power. Amun, seated on his throne, then crowns the kneeling king, who turns round so that the god can place his hand on the nape of his neck. Henceforth, Pharaoh, transfigured by these rites of passage, stands outside time. As he is told: "The whole length and breadth of the earth is given to you; none shares it with you."

Atum: Egyptian creator god. From his seed he brought forth the first divine couple, Shu and Tefnut, from whom the principal gods of ancient Egypt descend. Divinity of the Heliopolis region.

The establishment of the titulary

Cartouche of Ramses II.

THE MOMENT HAD COME to lay down the "protocol" formed by the five great names governing the program of his reign and drawn up by the royal scribe of the House of Life, Samut. The epithet "Mighty-Bull-Beloved-of-Maat" was selected as a "banner name" (the name of Horus) and inscribed in a picture of a palace enclosure dominated by the Horus falcon. Then, protected by the two tutelary mothers ("ladies") symbolized by the vulture and the cobra, he becomes "Protector of Egypt, Fetterer of Foreign Lands." Then comes the "Horus of Gold" title: he will be "Rich in years, great with victories." The last two names were each contained within an oval cartouche, the end product of the round *shenu* insignia, an allusion to the solar sphere. The first cartouche, preceded by the title "King of the South and North", contains a simple repetition of *Usermaatre*, "Powerful is the *maat* [the factor of cohesion and energy essential to universal harmony] of the Sun," to which in a very few years Ramses was to append the term *Setepenre* ("chosen by the sun"). The second cartouche contained Ramses, his birth name, as pronounced by his mother. Much later, the king would have it spelt *Ra-mes-su*.

The great name was then sent out by decree to the various provinces of the country. During the whole long ceremony, the liturgy exalts Ramses, who, imperceptibly, moves into another world. This is the moment chosen for the thousand-year-old heritage to be passed down to him.

The transmission of a millennial heritage

R AMSES WAS NOW TO BE ANOINTED with labdanum and have protective amulets placed around his neck, a ritual carried out this time to the sound of a hymn to Horus. At last the most significant act arrived: the communion. He had to swallow an edible symbolic image modeled in breadcrumb that alluded to the hieroglyphic sign for the word *function (iaut)*, which had previously been stamped onto his hand with a resin gum moistened with saliva. It was after this action that he was accorded the power to govern:

Iaut sign used to write the word "function," (originally conferred on Pharaoh by Atum).

"The iaut*-emblem of Horus is his.
Its power to govern belongs to him!"**

Then it was time to evoke the past of the preceding reign. A wafer had been made out of humus from the flood zone of the fields, again mixed with various mineral salts, while certain royal insignia designed to indicate the powers conferred on him were placed on Ramses' neck: images of a falcon, a bee, and scepters. Next, he was offered seven divine images from the House of Life of the temple, in clay and in animal form with a flame shooting out of their mouth.

Now, as night fell, Ramses had to undergo a kind of incubation, so that he might enter the new existence of his reign. A bed had been set up in the holy of holies, and four wooden seals had been given to the king: two in the name of Geb, one with the image of Neith, and the last bearing the name of Maat. These seals, it is written, were then "placed under the king's head as he lay"; Ramses had already entered a state of semi-torpor.

*Falcon-headed Horus
presents Ramses II with
the hieroglyph for* ankh,
*symbol of life.
From Abydos. Musée
du Louvre, Paris.*

After acting out the symbolic death, the "awakening" found Ramses in a strange, magical atmosphere. Most of all, the new sovereign was sitting on a "mysterious throne built on a stone," whose function was naturally prophylactic.* Ramses must have held the humus wafer in one hand and, in the other, most probably a swallow. Officiants would then have brought in the falcon of Horus. The swallow's role was to lay a curse on any who would harm Horus, while the falcon was to announce to Horus himself that his inheritance had indeed been transmitted. For protection to be accorded to the incumbent of a glorious new reign, one final rite had to take place: that of the destruction of all harmful forces, illustrated by the "decapitation" of two sets of seven plants. First, the king had to smell their fragrance, before cutting off each of their heads. He was then clad in a robe of red linen covered with prophylactic amulets.

Next, Ramses returned to the House of Life to receive an offering of nine live birds of different species, while a gold falcon, a vulture made of enameled frit, and a cat of turquoise were hung around his neck. Among the birds, we can identify a falcon, a vulture, a kite, a goose of the Nile, a *mesyt* bird, a swallow, a crane—all guardians. At the appropriate moment, the wings of the falcon, then those of the vulture, open out behind the back of the king's neck.

Prophylactic:
concerning a preventive
treatment that aims
to avoid the onset
of disease.

The *ished* tree and the longevity of Pharaoh

*Amun-Atum and
Seshat inscribe
the throne names
of Ramses on fruit
from the* ished *tree.
Ramesseum,
Thebes-West.*

THE IMPOSING SCENE OF THE crowning which took place in the secrecy of the temple was the most significant ritual of the entire royal existence and was, in its broad lines, reiterated on each New Year's Day, so as to ensure its continued effectiveness. For Ramses, the first stage must have taken place in Memphis. Most probably the liturgy would have been terminated at Heliopolis, in one of the sacred courts where the beautiful *ished* tree (persea) was tended. The Egyptians knew that the fruits of the persea that lined the canals ripened just before the arrival of the flood, like a welcome augury for New Year's Day.

One of the end points of the consecration thus consisted in inscribing the names and first names of the pharaoh on fruit from the sacred tree. Ramses would have sat on the ancient throne before the persea. Behind him stood an image of Atun, the self-begetting power, which ensured the perpetuity of his power on earth. Wielding a calamus,* the Master of Origins with noble gestures inscribed on one of the fruits he held up in his hand the throne name: User-maat-re Setep-en-re. Facing the king, Seshat, Mistress of the Writings and Sovereign of the Books—followed by Thoth, the divine intelligence—performed the same rite on another fruit, holding the Sign of the Jubilees promised for "millions of years" in the other hand.

Calamus: reed-pen trimmed to a point for writing.

Facing page:
*Harpist, sistrum-players
and acrobats take part
in the festival of Opet.
Relief from the Sanctuary
of the Boat of Hatchepsut.
Open-air Museum, Karnak.*

Leaving the sacred enclosure, the festival now radiated out over Egypt. The king doubtless took part in the public rites—slaying the wild bull, hunting down the vicious ostriches, firing arrows at distant, heavy targets, etc. Then he would have paraded on a gold-plated chariot, like the sun, in the midst of his people whose joy was further gladdened by the leniency shown by the new sovereign, who would take the opportunity of granting amnesties.

The great festival of Opet

GENERAL JUBILATION TOOK OFF again after the fortnight's holiday for New Year's Day, since, during this period when the rhythm of work slowed thanks to the beneficial influx of water over the fields, the festival of Opet was about to be celebrated in Thebes for twenty-three days. This was the occasion for all the residents to watch the sumptuous procession of the incredibly opulent sacred barque, bearing a representation of Amun, followed by two other barges dedicated to the goddesses Mut* and Khonsu,* the image of the son-god. The procession wended its way between the sanctuary of Karnak and that of Luxor farther south, where the master of Thebes was about to begin celebrating his hymen with his consort and the renewal of his *ka** during a festival in the temple that lasted more than eleven days. Traveling down the canal that runs parallel to the Nile and nearer the temple of Karnak, the divine vessels were placed on great river craft drawn by the faithful and members of the army: during the whole procession they were, of course, the object of admiration and devotion. The Great Priest of Amun had just died, and Ramses decided to lead the

Mut: goddess symbolizing maternal values, she is the wife of Amun. A dangerous divinity, she can be transformed into a lioness, but, in her manifestation as a vulture, she also watches over mankind and revives them. Divinity of the Theban region.

Khonsu: lunar divinity with the head of a falcon surmounted by a disc which fights against the forces of darkness by Pharaoh's side.

Ka: immaterial element that concentrates the vital energy of humankind and of the gods, it is in addition the incarnation of Pharaoh's divinity.

panegyrics himself. So he put on the cheetah skin worn by priests, but, in a gesture unique in the annals of Egypt, the written caption accompanying the scene illustrated gives him the title of "First Prophet of Amun, the King of the South and North [Countries], Ramses User-maat-re."

Henceforth, and for the first thirty years of his reign, the fiery young sovereign, his impetuous will further consolidated by his transfiguration at the crowning, was to lead a boundlessly active existence.

King and builder

PHARAOH, ACCOMPANIED BY Nefertari, who was blessed by the gods for having bestowed on him his eldest son, were to celebrate the feast of Min, the guarantor of good harvests. This was but an interlude, however: summoning his architects, Ramses ordered them to draw up plans for a gigantic court, its porticos lined with statues, encompassing shrines for the barques outside the temple at Luxor. An imposing pylon was to enclose the sacred precinct decorated with colossi and a pair of obelisks.

Soon Ramses envisaged marking the site of his future jubilee temple on land on the left bank of Thebes. To him the best place appeared to be located next to the small building which, shortly before the death of his father, he had planned to erect for his mother, Tuya, whom he now referred to as *Mut*-Tuya—a clever hint that his mother sprang from the divine companion of Amun.

The selection of a new high priest of Amun at Karnak

FOLLOWING THE DEATH OF Nebneteru, whose role had been performed by Ramses at the festival of Opet, it was urgent to appoint a new high priest. The entourage of the young pharaoh soon entered into the swing of the ritual selection of the candidates. Amun himself was meant to choose his highest functionary through an oracle, and he accepted the name of Nebwennef among all the dignitaries offered up. The elected official then had to quit his functions as high priest of Onuris at Thinis and of Hathor at Dendera, and instead use his skills to pilot Ramses' diplomatic plans at Karnak.

By now, the sacred barques were making their way back to Karnak by land routes dotted with shrines in which the crowds

Statuette of god Amun-Min. Musée du Louvre, Paris.

Facing page:
Entrance to the Temple of Amun, with two statues of a seated Ramses II and the obelisk. Luxor.

could gaze on the little boats deposited there, containing precious statuettes, materializations of divine and invisible forces. The heavy, shimmering barques were borne on stretchers by shaven-headed priests in long white linen robes, while opulently harnessed horses paraded in the cortège. Pharaoh was always escorted by Nefertari, while the royal children sat upon their own personal mini-chariots piloted by drivers placed under the authority of the royal shield-bearer, Imenemipet, a close friend of Pharaoh and future Master of the Horse.

Further constructions

UNABLE, DURING THIS CRUCIAL period, to inspect the full extent of his realm, Ramses appointed his viceroy in Nubia, Iuny, to embark on new building projects in the south of the country to commemorate his ascent to power. The new residence of the viceroys was now definitively confirmed: Aniba (Miam) in Lower Nubia would remain an urban repository of the wealth of Africa, but the authority of Pharaoh was to reach still further south, to Upper Nubia. The new capital of Amara, founded by Seti, was rapidly expanding. To the north of the Second Cataract, Ramses also ordered Iuny to select a favorable site for two sacred caves that would illustrate the indisputably divine nature of the royal couple and surpass the message of the temples of Soleb and Sedeinga in Sudan, over which still hovered the memory of Amenophis III and his sublime Tiyi. At Karnak, the works begun by Seti had been suspended since the king's death and the festivities surrounding the coronation, then those of Opet. Ramses, counting on skillful management from Nebwennef to stifle any outcry from the powerful ranks of the priesthood, now had them resumed as promptly as possible, so that the immense hypostyle could rapidly be used for the sumptuous rites of Amun.

The first acts of Pharaoh's reign

BEFORE LEAVING THEBES, Pharaoh gathered together his most important aids: the chief of the treasury, head tax collector and revenue inspector, and other senior officials, all selected among friends from his youth, some Asian in origin. He appointed Paser, his vizier, to inform him as to the total resources of the country and to the various grades of the vast civil service in

*Ramses, accompanied
by Nefertari, appoints
Nebwennef as high priest
of Amun at Karnak.*

his administration. Pharaoh also conferred one last essential task
on the man who was to serve as a major tool in his drive for equity:
a daily report to the sovereign on his management of affairs and on
the state of the river.

The early years of Ramses' rule

Ramses had been crowned at Memphis, the land of Ptah,
Master of the Jubilees; he had been consecrated at Thebes by
Amun himself, and the function of Atum had been confirmed on
him by the god of Heliopolis. It now remained for him to under-
line his presence as the incumbent of the seat of Horus, in the
majestic domain of Osiris, in Abydos, near the prestigious edifice
willed by his father and still under construction.

He also needed to complete the halls of the sanctuaries dedicated to the founder of the dynasty, Ramses I. Everything con-
spired to make Abydos into a crucial stopover on his return
journey north: did he not have to announce personally to the new
high priest of Amun, Nebwennef, the propitious utterance of the
oracle which had singled him out as Pharaoh's ally in the powerful
domain of Thebes? During this first year of his reign, Ramses,
with Nefertari, the royal family, the most senior members of the
court, and the Council of the Thirty constantly at his side, proclaimed, in the customary orotund language, the favored choice of
the god. The event, which marked the climax of Nebwennef's
career, was faithfully reproduced in his tomb, since he had been

chosen in preference not only to all the prophets of the gods and all the dignitaries of the House of Amun, but also to all the members of the court and to the Chief of the Soldiers.

The monuments of Abydos

A S HE MADE HIS WAY THROUGH the complex of buildings dedicated to Osiris, towards the (thousand-year-old) Staircase of the Great God, around which, for centuries, the steles of the faithful had accumulated, it must have dawned on Ramses that there could be no more favorable place of pilgrimage at which to leave a record of his history to posterity. He therefore decided to attribute the declarations recorded with such lavish praise in the dedicatory inscription—already mentioned in connection with his childhood—to his father; naturally enough, he also ordered that the building ordained by Seti be completed and the enacting of the rite there assured.

Yet he did not forget to found in this place of worship a temple of his own, built of limestone and splendidly decorated with delicate reliefs. Respectful of his father's memory, the son of Seti extended his devotion to the ancestors he desired to appropriate to his own ends. A further episode in his quest for legitimacy, he also did his utmost to renovate the ancient burial places of the earliest kings, which none of their descendants, it would seem, had taken care of. He set up a department to oversee the restoration work and to ensure the distribution of offerings. Much later, his example was followed by his son, Khaemwaset, an archaeologist at heart who made notable progress on the dilapidated antique monuments at the Necropolis of Sakkara and at Giza. Moreover, in the Temple of Seti, where the decorations for certain walls had

Below: Plan of Pi-Ramesse showing the principal quarters.

Below right: Staircase leading to the platform of the throne room in the Palace of Pi-Ramesse.

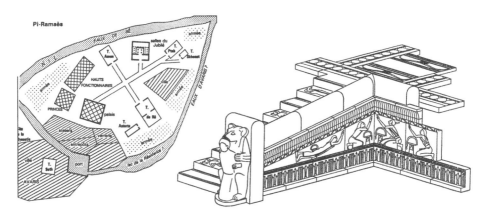

May, chief architect in the Temples of Re and Ptah. Egyptian Museum, Cairo.

not yet been completed, he made a point of having himself depicted as a child next to his father, before the impressive list of the ancestors of the crown—so as to further underscore his right to the throne.

Work at Pi-Ramesse

Back in Pi-Ramesse, where the extension work was gathering pace, Pharaoh summoned his architects and commanded them to place four majestic buildings at the heart of the city. To the north of the old southern town of Avaris, formerly occupied by Hyksos,* stood the Temple of Seth and the vestiges of the Temple of Seti, awaiting enlargement. Not far from there lay the port of the future capital, where the branch of the Nile called the "Waters of Re" in the west and the "Waters of Avaris" in the east joined and

Hyksos: multiethnic group living in western Asia which arrived to the east of the Nile delta in the course of the Second Intermediate Period.

crossed the "Lake of the Residence," to which memories of the naval battle between the liberator and the invaders remained attached. Pi-Ramesse, then, was surrounded by water. At the center of the new city, at the four ends of two broad intersecting arterial roads, Ramses ordered the construction of a palace and three sanctuaries: to the north, the Temple of Ptah, flanked by the building devoted to Sekhmet; to the east, a building for the worship of Amun; opposite this, to the west, the largest of the three shrines, the Temple of Re; and, to the south, the great palace, sheltered by a wide perimeter wall. Barracks were planned around almost the entire circumference. The person in charge of the architectural program, including the enlargement of the palace, was, it seems, the head builder, May, who had been a high-ranking soldier and whose career was to continue under Ramses at Heliopolis, then later under Ramses' thirteenth son, Merenptah. May must, then, have been very young when his talents brought him to the attention of Ramses. Extremely conscientious, he would accompany his workmen into the granite quarries of Aswan from which the majority of the obelisks for Pi-Ramesse were extracted. He seems to have been rather less respectful, however, when in all probability he purloined blocks from the cladding of the Pyramid of Khephren at Giza for monuments in the new capital.

There was also work to be done enlarging the superb gardens of which Ramses was so fond, planting new orchards with apples and pears from the Middle East. Soon, admiring poets were singing the praises of what became one of Ramses' favorite spots.

A hymn to the Nile

THE FLOOD SEASON WAS ABOUT to return at the end of the first year of Ramses' reign; it was the ideal occasion to devote a great anthem to the Nile designed to ensure its crucial and abundant reappearance. A great stele was placed in the rock face at Gebel Silsileh to the north of Aswan, at a place where the river, flanked by sandstone quarries, narrowed.

Monuments in Thebes

PASER REGULARLY SUBMITTED reports to Pharaoh, much to the latter's satisfaction. He could follow the extraction of the rocks from the Valley of the Kings as his tomb was dug at the place he had chosen at the time of his father's funeral. In the second year of his reign, the ritual first blow with the chisel—a splendid silver graver, in point of fact—had been made in the fine limestone. Ramses would also have learned that the enlargement of the temple at Luxor was nearing its end. The granite quarries of Aswan had also provided beautiful pink stone for the pharaoh's colossi.

The wall decorations were well advanced, and the religious scenes adorning the inner face of the First Pylon were already completed. The obelisks, including the one Mehemet Ali later offered to France, were about to be erected opposite the breakwaters, but the pylon frontage oriented towards Karnak, from where the great festival of Opet would come each year, was not yet historiated. The great road connecting the Temple of Karnak to the new façade at Luxor was to be redrawn, and the series of sphinxes lining this majestic processional way, already refurbished under Tutankhamun, was to be added to. Egypt, in fact, had been transformed into one vast building site.

A well for the miners in the deserts of Kuban

ONE OF THE MOST SIGNIFICANT pieces of news Pharaoh would have learnt in the third year of his reign was sent to him by the chief of the treasury, Nebit (appointed in the second year of his reign), and concerned the goldmines. Egypt was certainly enjoying a period of plenty, and the mines close to Wadi Hammamat between Edfu and the Red Sea yielded a plentiful harvest of the noble metal, thanks to improvements in the water supply that Seti I had ensured by having a well dug in this arid zone. He had then vainly tried to find water in Lower Nubia, at Wadi Allaki, on the route to other goldmines. Situated seventy-five miles (one hundred and twenty kilometers) south of Aswan, this wadi was fortified by a sturdy citadel whose importance had already been recognized during the Middle Kingdom.

Subsequently, under Tuthmosis III, the great conqueror had built a sanctuary to the Horus of Baki (Kuban), one of the four aspects of the Nubian Horus, the other three being Miam (Aniba), Buhen (Wadi Halfa), and Abu Simbel (Meha), where the divinized Ramses formed an incarnation of the local Horus. Once more Ramses was spurred on by the glory surrounding the victorious Tuthmosis III, and this site, too, was to bear his stamp. The temple had been set up on the left bank of the river: Ramses now raised a new religious building in the fortified enclosure on the right bank, where its ruins were later unearthed. His intention was clearly to carry on the work of his predecessors and to surpass the actions of his father: as a darling of the gods, he could force the gates of destiny…

After having the workmen bore down to one hundred and twenty cubits,* Seti had indeed been forced to halt the drilling. Ramses' viceroy suggested, therefore, that the providential sovereign reconsider the problem; success was sure to follow. A stele of great interest found in the nineteenth century near the village of Kuban, not far from the imposing fortress of Baki on the arid and formidable route to the goldmines, preserves an extremely informative text. True, it quite naturally testifies to a significant event in the economic history of the reign; but it also provides one of the most telling examples of the way in which acts attributed to Pharaoh could be exaggerated in eulogies and of the length to which such toadying could go. On this point, although grandiloquence in laudatory royal texts was very much the norm in the New Kingdom, Ramses remains unsurpassed.

The Kuban Stele

THE TERMS EMPLOYED ALSO presented Pharaoh with an opportunity to return to the favorite topic of his extraordinary precocity and to air the praise lavished upon it by loyal courtiers. Finally, another facet of his "self-advertising" comes across loud and clear: to present himself as a man of providence, as a miracle-worker. Where his father had been unsuccessful in detecting water at a depth of more than a one hundred and twenty cubits, *he* had only to turn his attention to the problem for it to be instantly solved. The Stele of Kuban constitutes the most characteristic example of the panegyric and political literature of the early part of our hero's reign.

(Rather more recently, another miracle has occurred. When sites for excavation were allotted among the various nations who had answered the appeal to save Nubia [before it was submerged beneath the waters of the Aswan Dam], our Russian colleagues chose Wadi Allaki and the site of Akata, concluding their investigations with the discovery of the vestiges of the famous well still bearing its name of Khenemet Ramses Meryamun, ken-nakht.)

It was certainly necessary to increase output from the goldmines in Nubia to enrich the treasury of Amun, but another motive probably prompted Ramses to speed up the process. Like his predecessors, the liberators of Egypt, he was committed to supporting the army in which he himself had served. Regular grants of land and rewards of gold offered the best guarantees of loyalty, all the more so since numerous divisions were composed entirely or in part of contingents from abroad, such as Libyan mercenaries, the Sherden, or the loyal Nubian archers.

The first Syrian campaign

IT WAS THE FOURTH YEAR of his reign, and Ramses had just turned twenty-nine. The dispatches sent by the king's informers in the Middle East (his "ears"), and assembled by his vizier, all concurred: since the treaty passed between Seti and the king of the Hittites, Muwatallis, the king of Amurru, Benteshima, seemed to harbor no fears of aggression from Egypt, since he was assured of support from his powerful, if rather remote, Hittite protector. Ramses, however, was little inclined to abandon what had been an Egyptian possession since the time of Tuthmosis III: the moment was ripe to recover the province and prepare to invade the city of Kadesh (Qadesh). Located on the Orontes, only slightly southeast of the Eleutheris, it was a strategic position of the highest importance, to the northeast of Byblos. At the head of his troops, Ramses moved up to Syria in the summer of 1275 BCE, ready to confront the Hittites of the land of Anatolia, the Khatti (or Kheta),* who continued to threaten Egypt and had already seized a number of Syrian cities within the protectorate of Pharaoh.

Khatti: indigenous inhabitants of the land of the Hittites.

He crossed the lands of Canaan, passed by Gaza, skirted Ascalon, and, leaving Mageddo inland to the east, marched to Tyre on the Mediterranean coast, pushing up to Byblos—all cities with Egyptian garrisons, which greatly facilitated his progress. He most probably subdued Irkata, where the Eleutheris disgorges into the sea, and penetrated farther east into the territory of Amurru, where he easily destroyed the forces of its king. Benteshima, it appears, was astonished by this lightning attack, and in short order found himself a vassal of Egypt, while secretly entertaining links with his former Hittite master and reassuring him of his rather ineffectual loyalty.

After thus preparing the ground—and imposing tribute on Benteshima—Ramses, now confident of his strategy, returned by way of Phoenicia. At Byblos, not far from the city he had founded on his way through and to which he had given the name of Pi-Ramesse ("the Valley of the Cedars"), he erected a stele in honor of his actions close to Nahr el-Kelb ("the River of the Dog"). Two other triumphal steles, including one near Tyre, were also erected, but unfortunately their texts are now rather the worse for wear.

Preparing the second Syrian campaign

ONE IMAGINES THAT, prior to leaving Amurru, Ramses, in readying his future expedition, would have stationed a contingent of well-trained recruits in Irkata, the Nearin, ready to join the main army when the time came to face the Hittites. Sixty days after his departure from Egypt, Ramses again passed by the fortress of Tjaru (Sila), before regaining his quarters on the verdant banks of the "Waters of Re." He was now to devote around five months to thinking through the expedition to retake the towns and confront the Hittites, an action that his youthful enthusiasm seemed to desire ardently.

For the flood season, the Great Royal Wives, Nefertari and Isisnofret, the queen mother Tuya—glowing with pride for a son who had already begun to walk so gloriously in his father's footsteps—the ladies in waiting, and the royal children had all repaired to the royal harem at Fayum. There, their preferred pastimes, enjoyed more freely than at court, included taking the air by Lake Karun (Mi-ur, the Moeris), hunting game-birds, fishing excursions, long boat trips, chariot races for the young princes, archery practice, and outdoor sports generally. The princes would also have visited the vineyards, very different from those on the delta, where presses produced a golden juice that was turned into sweet wine. As for the princesses, they had already been initiated into spinning and weaving at the great royal workshops directed by the queen mother, whose splendid garments dressed the royal family and which also produced the precious gossamer-like fabrics often presented to foreign sovereigns. But there was also work to do in readiness for the great expedition: Ramses would have surrounded himself with his intimate circle, keen to offer them the unforgettable spectacle of a defeated enemy.

He knew that, in preparation for the coming fight, his foe had been busy mustering his allies and vassals into a confederation, and had thereby raised a huge if rather miscellaneous and perhaps undisciplined army whose core—the only well-organized contingent—was formed by the Hittite chariotry. Muwatallis would have had to dig deep in his pocket to compose this military ragbag. Information reaching Ramses' ears spoke of two massive armies, each with twenty thousand men, while the Hittite cavalry included some two and a half thousand chariots.

But what forces lay at the disposal of Ramses, Pharaoh of all Egypt? Could he hope to be in a position to meet so formidable a coalition in just a few months? It seems that he for one was utterly convinced that he could.

Ramses' army

ADMITTEDLY, AT THAT TIME, Ramses could rely on a well-trained, professional army backed up by "hired" soldiers. An inspector of the military scribes was responsible for recording this force in the presence of His Majesty. The general staff surrounding Pharaoh, who remained the supreme commander of the army, was composed of generals-in-chief, princes of the blood, and qualified favorites, as well as some purely honorary generals.

The four infantry divisions

RAMSES' EXPEDITIONARY force, arrayed in readiness for the battle to retake the city of Kadesh, was composed of four divisions, each of which included approximately five thousand men. The division provided by the inhabitants of the north of the delta was placed under the banner of Seth, and that of the southern tip of the delta was under the banner of Re. Ptah served for recruits from the area of Memphis, while the Theban region provided the division of Amun and remained quartered in Upper Egypt, ready to intervene in particular in Upper Nubia (Sudan).

Supply corps and force composition

A WELL-APPOINTED SUPPLY CORPS was placed under the authority of civil servants, and each division was provided with one scribe for manpower and another for provisions. All were high dignitaries and were assisted by twenty military scribes in charge of both the soldiery and their supplies, and each catering for the needs of two hundred and fifty men.

Arsenal and bridgeheads

AN ARSENAL FOR MANUFACTURING and repairing the chariots was set up in a suburb of Memphis. Having protected itself from the Syrian threat at a time when Egypt was menaced by a new danger—the Hittites—the military stations and outposts on which Ramses was to rely, already partly restored by Seti, now straddled the road east. In first place an armory was placed in the fortress of Tjaru (Sile) on a line with el-Kantara on the border of the eastern delta.

Any expedition to the Levant would be forced to cross the border at this point, and again on the return, while a little to the south, the corridor through which the Asiatics would penetrate from northern Sinai was located at Wadi Tumilat. At this spot there stood the fortress of Tjeku (in Hebrew *Succoth*), the headquarters of the police responsible for monitoring the Bedouin tribes entering the delta to graze their herds. Following Seti's campaigns, over a length of some hundred miles, the road from the delta to Gaza was provided with approximately twelve fortified locales to protect the wells (*khenemet*).

There were also various kinds of headquarters. One such was Gaza, which controlled an area up to the plain of Asdralon. Another Egyptian headquarters was located in the valley of the Beka, to the north of Damascus. The grain stores of Jaffa were a significant center for the provision of the troops, and a chariot repository was established in the same place under the Ramessides. Last but not least, the fortress of Mageddo was responsible for overseeing the harvest from the plain of Asdralon.

The eve of the second Syrian expedition

IN THE FIFTH YEAR OF HIS REIGN, confident in the strength of an army that at last seemed well and truly "run in," Ramses, now in his thirtieth year, was preparing to cross the land of Canaan and make his way to where the Hittites awaited him at Amurru. His military concerns, however, did not mean he was neglecting the governance of his country. At the request of Vizier Paser, he nominated the scholar Ramose as scribe of the "Place of Truth" (at Deir el-Medina), thereby strengthening the administration of the precious royal necropolises of west Thebes.

Ramses, at this point, was about to embark on what is today cited as the first great battle of antiquity, the records of which, in the form of writings and imagery bequeathed primarily by Pharaoh himself, constitute a virtually "live" historical account.

Facing page:
Statue of the scribe Ramose.
Musée du Louvre, Paris.

3

THE BATTLE OF KADESH

Why Kadesh?

Mitanni: kingdom in the north of what is now Syria. This feudal state was led by an aristocracy who were originally warriors.

The council of war held by Ramses after the arrest of the Hittite emissaries. Hypostyle hall, Abu Simbel.

WHY KADESH? WHY WAS the confrontation between the armies of Pharaoh and the Hittite confederation of such importance? At stake was which of the two sovereigns, Muwatallis or Ramses, could position his country as the dominant power over the lands between the Tigris–Euphrates and the Mediterranean and thereby control trade, making himself, *ipso facto*, the mightiest of the time. Since the Eighteenth Dynasty, and in opposition to the Mitanni,* the pharaohs had endeavored to establish themselves in the Valley of the Orontes and especially in the citadel of Kadesh (modern Tell Nebi Mend), which commanded the routes to the Euphrates. The danger of the Mitanni had receded before the beginning of the Ramesside period: a peace had been forged once more by marriages between the pharaohs and the princesses of the country. The region was overseen at that time by Egyptian governors who superintended relations between all the local princes who contributed regularly to the crown's coffers.

This set-up was partly disturbed when, during the reign of Akhenaten, Egypt neglected its positions in Asia. Benefiting from this show of weakness, the Hittites, distant neighbors in Anatolia, began to engineer a role for themselves in the Middle East, which, composed of little more than remnants of city-states, remained in constant conflict. At the beginning of the reign of Ramses II, Muwatallis, who was the same age as Ramses, headed the Khatti. At his capital of Hattusha, he was much closer than Ramses to the areas where military operations were about to resume, and could thus assess the field of operations with great precision, a singular advantage over his Egyptian adversary. During Pharaoh's first campaign in Syria, Muwatallis, perhaps to lull Ramses into a false sense of security, had failed to intervene, so that Ramses came to believe that he was neglecting his interests. But in fact, Muwatallis was spending his time securing—"by threats or corruption"—the co-operation of more than a score of minor principalities in Asia Minor and northern Syria. Now a clash between two great kingdoms, each at the summit of its power, was inevitable, and the battle, long awaited by both antagonists, was to provide abundant material for the annals of their lands.

On the Egyptian side, Ramses ordered that the historical "Bulletin," a detailed record in a rather military style, be lodged in his main temples. Copies have been discovered on the walls of five of his sanctuaries: in Abydos, Luxor, at the Ramesseum, and two in Nubia—in the great Temple of Abu Simbel and in that of Derr. The Bulletin is illustrated with vast surfaces of bas-reliefs evoking the principal phases of the battle. These huge compositions, showing lively episodes from the fray and the exploits of Ramses himself, represent a genuine innovation compared to the old system of traditional portrayal, which, from its very beginnings, had been ornamentally distributed over registers that tended to fragment, as it were, the successive stages of the action. For the four metropolitan temples, this original record of the battle was supplied with an independent and much more detailed text (one which omits, however, a number of important details) of a more literary bent that was dictated in the ninth year of his reign, in all likelihood by Ramses himself, to a scribe of his named Pentaur.

Though the great temple at Abu Simbel is adorned with one of the most condensed and suggestive versions of the Bulletin, it harbors no version of the Poem. To date, three papyri preserve the memory of the text inscribed by Pentaur.

The battle of Kadesh as described in the "Poem of Pentaur"

Here are a few extracts from the Poem:

"Beginning of the victory of King Usermaatre-Setepenre Ramses II, son of Re, Ramses Meryamon....

"His Majesty was a lord full of youth ... active ... his powerful limbs ... his vigorous heart ... his strength like that of Montu ... perfect in appearance like Atum, his beauty was a delight to behold ... great with victories ... one did not know when he wished to fight; [he was] a solid wall for his army; their shield on the day of combat, a peerless archer. He is braver than hundreds together ... like a fire as it burns itself up ... a million men cannot stand before him ... unacquainted with fear ... like a wild lion in the valley of the animals of the desert; not speaking like a braggart ... saving his army in the day of battle ... bringing his followers back to their homes, and saving his infantry, his heart like a mountain of copper.... His Majesty left for the north, his infantry and his chariotry with him, and made good his departure in the fifth year, the second month of the season of the summer [end of May], on the ninth day. His Majesty passed the fortress of Tjaru, as powerful as Montu in aspect, all the foreign lands trembled before him, and their chiefs brought their tributes.... The army skirted the narrow defiles, as if following a road in Egypt....

"His Majesty arrived near the town of Kadesh, and while the wretched, vanquished of the Khatti had come and gathered all the foreign lands up

Facing page:
Harpe* of Ramses II. Musée du Louvre, Paris.

§ **Harpe**: stick or crook showing that Pharaoh leads his people like a shepherd.

to the borders of the sea.... [But] there was none left of the money he had coined from his property and given to foreign lands to get them to come and fight with him.... Now, the wretched, vanquished of the Khatti, together with the many foreign nations which were with him, joined together and stood ready northeast of the town of Kadesh, but His Majesty was alone, with by his side his suite....

But the wretched, vanquished chief of the Khatti was in the midst of his army which was with him, but did not fight for fear of His Majesty. However, he had thrown forward men and horses exceeding the multitude like [grains of] sand: there were three men on only one chariot equipped with weapons and the instruments of war. They had been gathered together in ambush behind the town of Kadesh, and now they arrived on the southern side of Kadesh and cut the army of Re down the middle as it arrived: it no longer knew where it should prepare to join battle. This is why the infantry and charioteers of His Majesty were crippled, while His Majesty was north of the town of Kadesh on the western bank of the Orontes. His Majesty was sent word of the attack.

"Then His Majesty arose in glory like his father Montu; he took up the panoply of battle and girt himself with his corselet. He looked like Baal in his hour; the great team of steeds that transported His Majesty were named Victory-in-Thebes and belonged to the great stable of Usermaatre-Setepenre, beloved of Amun.

"Then, all alone and none with him, His Majesty galloped off and rushed into the horde of the vanquished of the Khatti. And His Majesty started to look about him and saw two and a half thousand chariots surrounding him, made up of the best warriors from the vanquished of the Khatti and of the many foreign regions that were with them...."

Ramses then addresses the god Amun:

"Is it good for a father to turn away from his son? Have I ever erred towards you?... I have never disobeyed your commands! What do you care, O Amun, for these vile Asiatics, so ignorant of God? Have I not erected many monuments to you, and did I not fill your temple with my spoils?... Do right by one who puts himself in your hands!

"I called upon you, my father Amun, when I was in the midst of multitudes I did not know. All the foreign lands were ranged against me ... being alone ... nobody with me, my numerous infantry having given me up and none of my charioteers seeking me!... I ceased calling them, for none heard.

"I found more succor in Amun than in thousands of infantrymen, than in hundreds of thousands of charioteers and even in ten of thousands of brothers and children of a single heart!... O Amun, I never exceeded your bidding. And behold, I prayed at the borders of foreign lands and my *voice reached the town of Heliopolis in the south. I found Amun when I called him.... He calls me from behind, as if we faced one another: 'I am with you, I am your father, my hand is with you. I am more succor than hundreds of thousands of men. I am the lord of victory!'...*

"I once again found my heart strong, and [felt] joy in my breast ... I was like Montu. I fired to my right and took prisoners to my left! In their eyes, I was like Sutekh [Seth] in action. I saw the two and a half thousand chariots, in the midst of which I found myself, laid low before my team. I sowed death in their mass as I desired. Whosoever among them fell was never to rise again.

"But the wretched chief of the Khatti stood amid his infantry and his charioteers, gazing on His Majesty as he fought, all alone, with neither his infantry, nor his chariotry ... He summoned many chiefs, each one with his chariots equipped with weapons of war.... Their total numbered one thousand chariots which launched themselves into the fire. I headed for them, being like Montu, and forced them to feel the strength of my hand and in an instant brought carnage among them as they were struck where they stood. One of them, calling out to his comrade, said: 'This is no man among us, but great Sutekh full of strength, Baal in person!... Let us flee before him, and save our lives while we can [still] breathe!...'

"His Majesty pursued them like a griffon. I killed [many] among them and did not cease!

Abu Simbel. Ramses charges the Asians. (From Prisse d'Avennes, Histoire de l'art égyptien, *1878, Bibliothèque des Arts Décoratifs, Paris.)*

"I raised my voice to call up my army, saying: 'Hold fast! Be of heart, my army, so you can admire my victory! Alone, [for] Amun was my guardian!

"How faint are your hearts, my charioteers! Not one is any longer to be trusted among you. Is there a single one of you for whom I would not have done a worthy deed? Did I not appear as a master while you were poor... But behold!... Not a man among you stood firm and held out a hand to me while I fought.... The crime my infantry and my charioteers have committed is greater than words can say. See, Amun gave me victory, while no infantry, no chariotry was with me.... I was alone, no senior officer followed me, no charioteer, no soldier of my army, no captain. The foreign lands which beheld me will pronounce my name far into uncharted regions!... All those who fired in my direction, their arrows missed their mark just as they were to touch me....

"Then my army began to praise me.... My senior officers set to magnify my powerful arm, and my chariotry proud of my renown declared: 'What an excellent warrior, he revives the heart! You saved your infantry and your chariotry! You are the son of Amun ... You devastated the country of the Khatti by your powerful arm....'

"Thus spoke His Majesty to his infantry, to his senior officers, and in the same way to his charioteers: ... 'Does not a man grow in his city when he returns having acted as a brave man in the presence of his lord?... In your heart of hearts, did you not realize I am an iron wall? What will people say when they hear that you abandoned me, alone, with nobody, and

Ramses II on his chariot. Bas-relief in the Temple of Ramses II, Abu Simbel.

A ring set with horses, materializing Ramses' vow that he would always provide them with a daily feed. Musée du Louvre, Paris.

that no senior officer, captain, or soldier came to my side to hold out his hand to me while I fought? I overcame millions of foreign lands, alone [with] my team: Victory-in-Thebes and Mut-is-Satisfied, my mighty steeds. It is in them I found succor when I was alone, combating so many foreign countries....

"At this juncture, the wretched chief of the Khatti sent [a message] that paid homage to my name as that of Re, saying: 'You are Sutekh, Baal in person. Your terror is a firebrand in the earth of the Khatti.' Then he dispatched his envoys bearing a letter in their hands, with the great name of His Majesty, addressing greetings to His Majesty of the dominion of Re-Horakhty....

"'Your servant speaks and makes it known that you are the son of Re, come out of his body. He has given you all the lands, joined together in one place. As for the lands of Egypt and the land of the Khatti, they are with you, they are under your feet. Re, your noble father, gave them you.... Behold, your power is great, your strength weighs heavy on the land of the Khatti. It is good that you killed your servants, your fierce face turned towards them, and that you showed no mercy! Behold, yesterday you passed by, killing hundreds of thousands. Today you came and left no heirs. Be not severe in your actions, victorious king! Peace is better than fighting, let us live!'

"Then My Majesty was lenient, like Montu in his time, when his attacks hit home. Then My Majesty ordered that all the chiefs of my infantry be brought to me, my charioteers, and all my senior officers, gathered together in one place, so they should hear the contents of what had been written to me. My Majesty made them listen to these words that the wretched chief of the Khatti had written to me. Then they said with one voice: 'Peace is extremely good, O lord, our Master! No blame should be attached to a reconciliation when it is your work, for who could resist you in the day of your ire?'

"Then My Majesty ordered that these words be heard and I made a peaceful withdrawal in a southerly direction. My Majesty returned from there in peace to Egypt with his infantry and his chariotry, all life, stability, might and main being with him.... Having reached Egypt in peace with Pi-Ramesse-Beloved-of-Amun-Great-with-Victory, and remaining in his palace ... the gods of his country came to him, honoring [him] and saying: 'Welcome, our beloved son, king of Upper and Lower Egypt, Usermaatre-Setepenre, son of Re, Ramses Meryamon....'

"They gratified him with millions of sed *festivals, for always on the throne of Re, all the foreign lands and all the countries prostrating themselves beneath his sandals for all eternity, without end."*

The battle of Kadesh as described in the military Bulletin

THE EXAGGERATED ANGUISH of the abandoned chief, desperate but determined to overcome; the intoxication of victory; the final bitterness—all this is found in this text dictated by Ramses to his scribe Pentaur four years after the incredible day of battle. The episodes of the informers, full of what we would today call "spin," have been deliberately expunged from the account. Ramses, of course, knew full well that they would hardly have enhanced his glory and would only have underscored his unconscionable imprudence. Dated to the day of the confrontation, the Bulletin was inspired by military witnesses who will certainly have lived through these terrible hours. The sober and laconic text is accompanied by illustrated commentaries that refer to real-life incidents. Closer to real events, such documents provide an opportunity to reconstitute the day of Kadesh in its broad outlines and incorporate less bravura incidents knowingly overlooked in the Poem.

The departure of the army

IN THE VANGUARD OF THE AMUN division, Pharaoh was preceded by his senior officers flanking a great pole topped by a ram's head, the insignia of the first division, firmly affixed to the first vehicle. The two and a half thousand men of the division would have followed immediately behind. Pharaoh was surrounded by his cup-bearers, who formed part of his escort together with the Sherden, his personal guard. The vizier—whose name is nowhere mentioned—was also present, together with the general staff, who are likewise not named. The family will have been represented on the expedition by his elder sons. At the time of the attack on the camp, the name of a royal wife is mentioned: Mutnofret. Could this be a scribal error for Isisnofret, the second Great Royal Wife? It seems instead that this Mutnofret belonged to the "travel harem" as a favored secondary wife, since the text specifies that the royal children and those of Mutnofret are to be kept out of

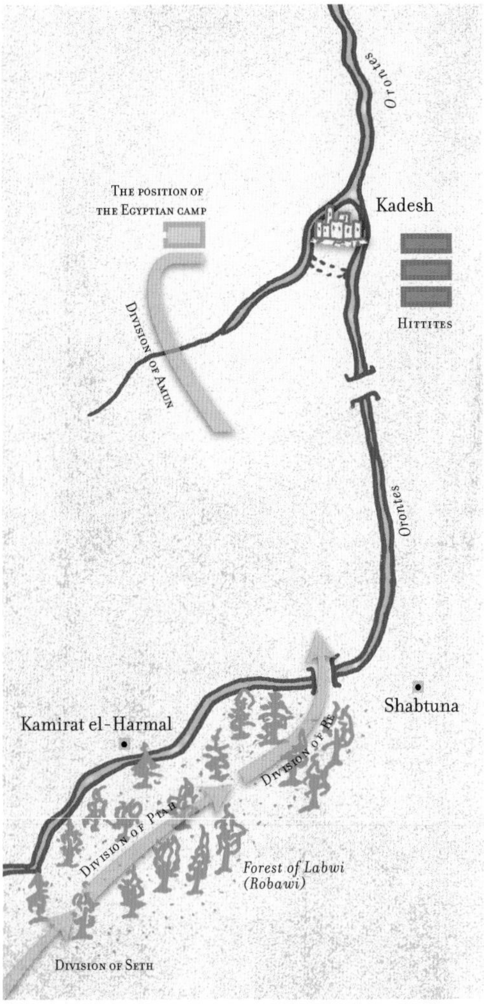
Orontes
The position of
the Egyptian camp
Kadesh
Hittites
Division of Amun
Orontes
Kamirat el-Harmal
Shabtuna
Division of Re
Division of Ptah
Forest of Labwi
(Robawi)
Division of Seth

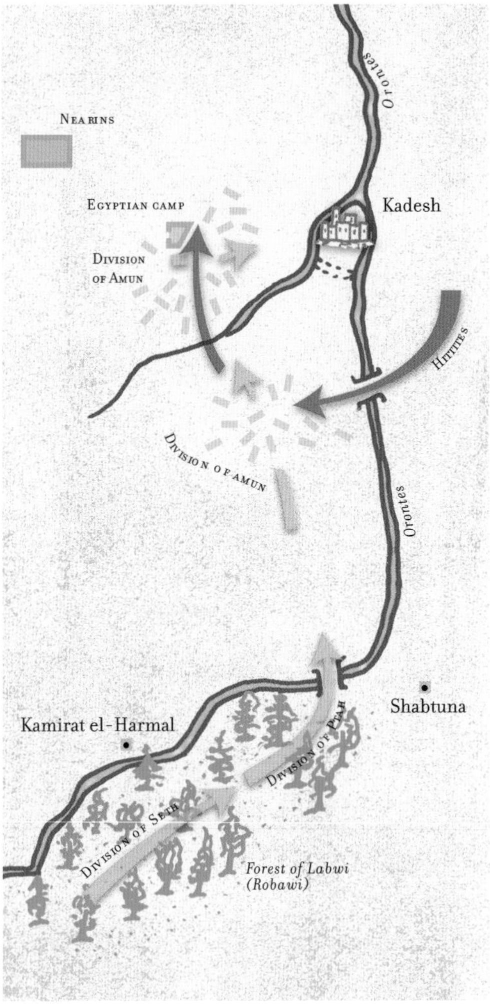
Orontes
Nearins
Egyptian camp
Kadesh
Division
of Amun
Hittites
Division of Amun
Orontes
Kamirat el-Harmal
Shabtuna
Division of Ptah
Division of Seth
Forest of Labwi
(Robawi)

Above:
The movements of the four Egyptian divisions prior to the Hittites' attack.

Above right:
Position of the four divisions at the time of the attack.

harm's way. Behind the division of Amun came that of Re, followed by that of Ptah, with the division of Sutekh (or Seth) bringing up the rear of the long military procession.

From the carefully noted dates we discover that the task force took a month to the day to reach the outskirts of the city of Kadesh. The supply corps assigned to each division was in charge of basic foodstuffs and bivouac material that was laden onto low-slung carriages drawn by bovines and asses.

Ramses traveled along the coast, perhaps beyond Tyre, towards Byblos. From there, he communicated with the Nearin forces, the elite of the army which he had set up a few months previously in readiness for his return. He then probably sent them to the mouth of the Eleutheris more to the north, so that a little later they could skirt the river in the direction of Kadesh, not far from its source. The two armies came together on the appointed day. Abandoning the coast, the army had to head between Lebanon and the Anti-Lebanon, in the depression of the Beka, arriving not far from Damascus and the administrative post founded by Ramses and named Pi-Ramesse-of-the-Valley-of-Cedars, in Amurru, and leaving the "vassals of Canaan" far behind. The division of Amun reached the final mountainous summits on the eastern bank of the Orontes and spent the night before the battle on a spot that today bears the name of Kamirat el-Harmal.

An enemy trick

THE NEXT MORNING, RAMSES, clad for war (wearing the "panoply of Montu") and impatient to move up to Kadesh, led his division through the straggling forest of Labuy. He wanted to cross the ford on the Orontes to the south of the town of Shabtuna as fast as possible, so as to advance to the right bank of the river about twelve and a half kilometers from Kadesh.

His scouts then spotted some men who seemed to be trying to keep out of sight: apprehending them, they noted they were both Bedouin, from the tribe of the Shasu. They introduced themselves as delegates from their group forming part of the Hittite coalition, but eager to escape from under the oppression of Muwatallis. According to them, "the vanquished of the Khatti [was] in the land of Aleppo, north of Tunip, and he [feared] Pharaoh too much to venture south."

Ramses had no idea that this was a maneuver dreamt up by Muwatallis, whose armies, numbering some twenty thousand men and including two and a half thousand charioteers, were actually massed not far from Pharaoh, to the northeast of Kadesh, concealed behind the citadel. A plan of battle must have immediately flashed through Ramses' mind: by driving up to the much-coveted fortress, rendered more vulnerable by the absence of Muwatallis and his army and defended apparently only by the Hittite force stationed at Aleppo, he might without great difficulty surprise and take it. What a brilliant revenge, and what glory for Pharaoh, who would appear all-conquering in the eyes of the entire Middle East! Hoodwinked by the prize dangled before him, Ramses was deaf to the dictates of reason and threw caution to the winds. He was intent on seizing it first with his own division, leaving the other three to join him later, once the stronghold had been victoriously stormed. So he hastened off with just the division of Amun in his wake and sped across the ford at Shabtuna, so as to march back by the left bank of the Orontes and reach the northwest of Kadesh.

Setting up the royal camp

O NCE ON THE SITE OF THE "bivouac" chosen by Pharaoh, the men, under the command of their officers and the scribes of the supply corps, proceeded to organize the camp and erect the royal tent adorned with the image of the foreign lands on their knees paying worship to the king. A huge rectangular area was immediately marked off by a light palisade of shields running all round the periphery. The entrance to the camp, in the middle of the west side, was flanked by two uprights topped with statuettes of recumbent lions that the supply corps had made sure were repro-

The camp of the division of Amun, established west of the town of Kadesh. The terrain is marked out with shields stood on their ends. The entrance to the left is adorned with two small sphinxes. The entire left section of the camp illustrates the daily life of the soldiers with the animals at rest (including His Majesty's lion undergoing training). On the right in an enclosure are the great tent of the king and three smaller tents for the princes. The Hittite attack encircles the royal tent. Top right, Pharaoh's emissaries order the royal family to be evacuated.

duced on the equipment of the royal train, for it was important to have the force of symbols on your side.

This entrance gave on to the main pathway through the camp, which traversed an area filled with men, animals, and material, as well as many smaller tents. This central avenue led directly to the royal marquee, rectangular in form with a round top, and to three small tents that will certainly have been used by the royal princes. Life in camp must have been a lively affair; to the east, however, the picture was abruptly turning into tragedy.

Let us imagine, for the moment, the western part of the main enclosure, where the different elements of the division of Amun thought themselves in perfect safety. To begin with, the entrance would have been marshaled by guards armed with pikes, while close by would be rows of horses out of harness, some in front of their feeding-troughs, others standing between the rows of chariots. Further along, asses used for transport would be grazing, lying on the ground, or perhaps being chastised by a passing soldier. Children reared by the camp followers flitted among the men

assigned to deal with the materiel and victuals, and would assist in bandaging the animals, maintaining the weaponry, inspecting the chariots, preparing meals, or treating the "walking wounded."

In the center, or thereabouts, a great recumbent lion, his tongue lolling out, is dubbed "the living lion of His Majesty, he who rips out the throats of his enemies." In front of him, his tamer was perfecting his training. In contrast to this scene of calm activity and repose, suddenly, a shudder of movement runs through the soldiers to the east: the men-at-arms start up, holding their shields before them; others turn to attack the Hittite charioteers who flood into the camp, overwhelming the eastern palisade. Some have already tumbled from their vehicles: Pharaoh's men hack them to pieces. Here, a royal officer on his chariot surges forth, extending his arm as if to issue an order. He is preceded by two other chariots mounted by princes and galloping at full speed westwards. What can have happened?

The consequences of the trick

T HE TWO SHASU, AGENTS PROVOCATEURS whose job had been to pull the wool over Pharaoh's eyes, had led him to the brink of catastrophe. The impetuous but inexperienced Ramses, in his overwhelming desire to garner a quick victory, never foresaw such an underhand blow. The enemy, massed to the northeast of Kadesh and keeping out of harm's way behind the citadel and in the surrounding vegetation, was to attack on two fronts—not only the camp, but the second division (that of Re) as well, just as it was passing the ford of Shabtuna and preparing to join up with the first army of Amun.

While the camp was still being organized, however, Ramses had been informed that two enemy reconnaissance scouts had just been intercepted in the vicinity. Soundly beaten, they ended up confessing the tragic truth to Pharaoh who questioned them: "[We] belong to the chief of the Khatti; it is he who sent us to spy on His Majesty's position." Ramses's reaction was once again immediate, and the celerity he showed faced with what was a dramatic situation testifies

Under his tent in the camp of the division of Amun, Ramses calls an urgent meeting with his vizier and officers. On the lower register, Egyptian Sherden and infantrymen stand either side of the Hittite emissaries while they are beaten.

to unquestionable courage and presence of mind: he at once convened his staff and informed them of the fearful disaster that now loomed over them.

This was obviously no time to point the finger at the negligence of his intelligence services, thought his council recognized its shortcomings, calling them "a great crime." He urgently dispatched the vizier, accompanying the young prince Pareherwenemef, First Champion of the Army and Master of the Horse, and messengers to Shabtuna and ordered the division of Ptah to make all haste. The latter was perhaps still partly waylaid in the wood of Labuy. The division of Seth was not worth mentioning, as it was too far away. As for the division of Re, Ramses thought it would be ready to join that of Amun, close to the camp.

Meanwhile, Muwatallis had launched the offensive, keeping before him some ten thousand infantrymen and sending two and a half thousand chariots each mounted by three occupants (a driver, a rider, and an archer) in the direction of the Orontes, crossing the ford nearest to Kadesh and meeting the Egyptians on the western bank of the river. Soon his soldiers would try to overrun the camp of Pharaoh. This, then, was the start of the great battle of Kadesh: an encounter lasting barely a day, but that Ramses turned into a watershed event and which remains the best documented military engagement before Marathon in 490 BCE.

Abu Simbel, painted reliefs in the great temple: the battle of Kadesh. (From Jean-François Champollion, Monuments de l'Égypte et de la Nubie, *1835.)*

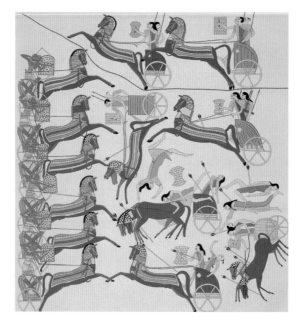

The fray

R AMSES WAS UNAWARE THAT Muwatallis' charioteers had just passed the Orontes and had literally split in two the column formed by the division of Re, whose elements now lay open to an attack as violent as it was unexpected.

The soldiers and cavalry, in their effort to escape the attackers, poured in disarray towards the camp of Ramses, surrounded by the division of Amun. Though confined to the inner circle, the council of war called by Ramses had barely finished deliberating when, alerted by the sound of arms close by, Pharaoh had his family evacuated, managed to muster his personal guard, and called up his shield-bearer, Menna, who had his chariot prepared. With lightning speed, Ramses entered the fray. Screaming a heartfelt war-cry, and sure of the steadfastness of his shield-bearer, Menna, who had managed to overcome his fear in face of an unimaginable and hopeless engagement, Ramses pushed himself to the brink of his limits. With complete confidence in the divine light that blazed in him, but goaded too by anger, he loosed arrow after arrow, passing the chariot reins round his back so as to leave Menna's hands free to pass him the arrows as he covered him with his shield. The despairing, almost blind, charge was indeed led by a demon! "This is no mere man!" howled his adversaries, as if paralyzed or in the grip of death.

The Nearin arrive

R AMSES LAUNCHED NO FEWER than six counter-offensives. He was on the point of being utterly engulfed, when suddenly gaps opened up in the enemy ranks. For there now appeared, emerging from the west in the direction of the camp, the magnificent contingent of the Nearin, whose arrival had been so brilliantly planned by the king. Comprised of hardened veterans—their marching order alone bespoke their discipline—the serried square of soldiers advanced in close formation, like a steamroller, shield against shield (a prefiguration of the Roman "tortoise"), flanked by chariots and ready to join arms. Gripping the enemy chariots encircling Ramses in a pincer movement, they wrestled the reckless pharaoh free, just as he was about to be overrun for good. In the same manner, the camp, too, already prey to plundering, was in part relieved. Pursuing the enemy to the northeast of the citadel, bolstered by the Nearin—a veritable "commando" of legionaries—and guided by Pharaoh, the

Following pages:
Ramses II's campaign in Syria. Battle of Kadesh. Ramesseum, Luxor.

Ramses II on his chariot fighting the Hittites. Ramesseum, Luxor.

Egyptian cavalry that was still fighting gathered together the scattered remnants of the division of Re, which was now joined by the division of Ptah, that had finally caught up after a forced march headed by the vizier. The scene was set for the opposing cavalry forces to rip into one another.

The reliefs illustrating the main episodes of the Bulletin depict the clash in a splendid middle register, with a lower section showing the Egyptian camp and the "council of war" presided over by Ramses. The upper register, on the other hand, portrays the appalling mêlée around Pharaoh and near the citadel of Kadesh, with a mass of broken chariots and corpses of both men and horses. Then comes the final phase of the combat: the victorious cavalry charge led by Ramses against the Hittite chariots hemmed in to the south of Kadesh, not far from the ford the Hittites had crossed in the other direction shortly before.

The Egyptian cavalry charge

POSITIONS WERE REVERSED, and now it was Ramses who had the upper hand. The Hittite chariots crossed back over the ford, but, above all, chariots, horses, and warriors were driven into the river (the majority of them drowning there) in total disarray.

These details are illustrated in the often tragic but sometimes amusing bas-reliefs taken from life, and they remained deeply engraved in the memories of Pharaoh's combatants. The record they provide, visible to all and displayed to a throng of visitors on the pylons at Luxor and the walls of Karnak—and even in sanctuaries, so that their iconographic power might perpetuate the victory—cannot have been based on lies.

Picturesque anecdotes are rendered with incredible verve. The artists—and the figures who inspired them—try to draw the viewer into the desperate fever of combat, to make him share in the emotion of critical situations, all the while savoring the details of daily life. The result is a masterpiece which owes a great deal to the "liberation" of the arts quite literally imposed by Akhenaton.

Following the thunderous charge towards the waters of the Orontes, the fate of the battle had definitively changed camp. In this unparalleled confrontation, Ramses' desperation and determination had undeniably proved to be assets.

Why, though, did Muwatallis, throughout the conflict, cling so obstinately to his infantry—who were on the left bank, but to the east of Kadesh—and never take part in the attack? Why, moreover, did he not unleash the immense forces of his infantry at the critical juncture when his cavalry was being forced back towards the Orontes? Was this man of Anatolia, accustomed to diplomatic

Ramses II charges the Asians.

Ramses II crushes his enemies. Great Temple, Abu Simbel.

maneuvers that generally culminated in treaties, determined to put a stop to a pointless carnage? Or was he heartbroken at the death of certain brothers, and others close to him, killed on the field? Or was he already afflicted by the disease that was to carry him away in the prime of life?

The end of the combat

MUWATALLIS CAN BE SEEN ON the reliefs illustrating the Bulletin, standing on his chariot to the southeast of Kadesh: his driver holds the reins of both horses, and he is surrounded by Hittites armed with pikes, the one in the vanguard wielding the characteristic violin-shaped shield. In front of the horses can be seen other warriors from the confederation, almost all from lands close to Anatolia, as we learn from the names of the regions they hailed from. The men brandishing large shields with rounded tops similar to those of the Egyptians must have come from countries that were one-time vassals of Pharaoh. Muwatallis, grasping the horses' reins as if to check his chariot, turns towards the citadel and raises his other hand in an effort to stop the battle. Perhaps he thought his troops should return to the citadel before the armies of Pharaoh tried to seize it? Or was he simply overwhelmed at the loss of so many of those close to him in the fray?

Orders, then, were given to the Hittite army to withdraw to the citadel. The stronghold, which was partly skirted by a large arm of the Orontes linked to a small canal, was surrounded by wide moats. These were spanned by two drawbridges, one in the south, another to the east. The soldiers of the confederation poured in behind Muwatallis, and the drawbridges were raised.

The evening after battle

Ramses has sometimes been accused of excessive boastfulness concerning the "triumph" at Kadesh. If, on the one hand, the poem overdoes the utter solitude of Ramses in the fray, the official reliefs of the Bulletin—and their commentary—provide a more truthful picture. The orders issued to the draughtsmen to coordinate the illustrations of the Bulletin between the various temples were strictly followed. The arrival of the Nearin and the register showing the engagement between the two opposing forces of charioteers deliberately underline the fact that Ramses was far from alone on the battlefield. In addition—and this can be seen at a single glance—it is obvious that the intention was to show that the citadel had *not* been taken, since, in the midst of the Hittite soldiers armed with pikes on the summits of the higher towers, the enemy standard flutters untouched; it is not pierced by enemy arrows, as will be seen at the time of the capture of Tunip in the eighth year of Ramses' reign.

On the Egyptian side, the division of Ptah, after finally making it to the battlefield, was joined by that of Seth even later, and did not fight. It remained to collect up the casualties, gather in the chariotry, bandage the horses, bring out the Egyptian dead, and count the number of

Above left:
The thousands of Hittite infantrymen Muwatallis held back from the battle.

Above center:
The citadel at Kadesh, skirted by two arms of the Orantes.

Above right:
The king of the Hittites orders his troops to lay down their arms.

On the evening after the battle, Ramses has the enemy dead counted (scribes record each left hand taken). The royal princes bring in prisoners. The vizier and the officers offer praise to Pharaoh.

enemy slain. To keep tally of the latter, the custom was to sever a hand from each enemy corpse and have it conscientiously recorded by scribes. These are piled up in macabre heaps before Pharaoh, while his sons and some senior officers present him with rows of vanquished chiefs, crestfallen *maryans* from several countries—the higher class, that is, of the most valorous charioteers. The king is seated on the cushion of his chariot, receiving the proof of his victory. In the lower register, his eldest son, now called Imenherkhepeshef (so named for the first time at the end of the battle), leads in the most important group of prisoners, their arms tied. In the middle register, the praises addressed to the king are illustrated by the vizier and the three major-generals, their arms raised in acclamation. The top register shows two princes bringing in another line of tethered prisoners and Hittite horses.

The senior officers and the vizier, because of their improvidence and their temporary absence from the battle, seem to have been punished by being left nameless. As for the king's sons, eight in number, they are all represented and named. The dressing-down addressed to his panic-stricken soldiers, as consigned in the pseudo-poem, must have been given during this ceremony at the end of the battle and will have contrasted with the praises handed out, for his unflinching support, to his shield-bearer, Menna. Nor did Ramses overlook the brave steeds of his team, "Victory-in-Thebes" and "Mut-is-satisfied," as is recorded in the Poem.

"Peace is better than combat" (Muwatallis)

ALTHOUGH THE TERMS OF THE POEM make it seem that Pharaoh wanted to resume the battle the very next morning, it appears that this assumption is without foundation. The taking of Kadesh must have appeared improbable to Ramses, whose four divisions were no longer intact (they could, of course, have been reinforced by assistance from the Nearin, but the latter will certainly have suffered losses of their own). The twenty thousand defenders of the citadel would have surely pinned attackers down in a prolonged siege. As we have seen, the Hittite, probably in a state of considerable distress, would have wanted to try the arm of diplomacy. The Poem reports the message sent by Muwatallis to Ramses, and the decision taken almost immediately by Pharaoh, after consulting with his senior officers and personal guard. Rejecting any further recklessness, the cost of which was all too evident to him now, Pharaoh judged that Muwatallis' olive branch would enable him to put an end, without losing face, to a confrontation he would certainly have regarded as perilous. Ramses took advantage, then, of the way-out offered him and proclaimed his "peaceful withdrawal" to the south.

The return to Egypt

As one might expect, messengers had been sent posthaste to the capital, and Ramses and his troops, with a number of prisoners in tow, but little in the way of booty, were given a heroes' welcome. Their praises were sung, and the lack of booty discreetly passed over, the spoils consisting mainly of weapons taken from the enemy dead and horses. All reference to the equipment destroyed when Ramses' camp was overrun was eschewed.

Ramses, however, remained completely lucid, having clearly understood how weak alliances forged with the princelings of the Middle East could be. It was a lesson he never forgot. He also knew that his return, after such a triumphal departure that had trumpeted the overwhelming power of Pharaoh, would be pored over and weighed up by his more belligerent neighbors, especially as Kadesh and Amurru remained in Hittite hands. He had to "get back in harness" quickly and return east as soon as possible to impose his will, retake the areas he had forfeited, reinstate Egyptian influence, and even try to consolidate, once again, its borders.

Upon the departure of the Egyptian army, Muwatallis had retaken Amurru. It was at this time that his chief Benteshima was exiled to the capital, Hattusha, and replaced in his fiefdom by a certain Shapilli. Muwatallis, meanwhile, grabbed Damascus, together with its province.

At Pi-Ramesse, Ramses set about redesigning the training program for his divisions and completely overhauling his intelligence services. Falling for the Hittite trick had shaken him deeply.

4

RAMSES,
THE BUILDER-KING

Facing page:
*Head of one of the colossal statues on the
façade of the Great Temple, Abu Simpel, Thebes-West.*

The immediate consequences of Kadesh

I MENHERKHEPESHEF, THE KING'S eldest son, had proven his worth during the engagement at Kadesh, and Ramses knew he could leave him in charge while he traveled to the south of the country. Moreover, the prince was much attached to two of the most faithful and effective servants of Pharaoh, on whom he placed great reliance. First, there was Vizier Paser, who had very probably stayed behind in the capital of the north to manage the affairs of the kingdom. Then there was Imeneminet, the epitome of intelligence and honesty, whom Pharaoh had just made head of the secret service, monitoring plots hostile to Egypt in the foreign territories.

The eastern border had been reinforced, so temporarily forestalling the fearsome Shasu, Bedouin fond of pillaging. These immediate preventive measures were followed by a cleansing of the upper echelons of the army, and then by a "rethink" in troop training (including the chariot officers), with a view to instilling stricter fighting discipline. Prince Imenherkhepeshef, appointed to apply the necessary reforms, was doubtless assisted in this role by General Urhiya, whose son had taken part in the battle of Kadesh at his side. In all events, Ramses knew that, during his absence from the capital, the queen mother, Tuya *Mut*-Tuya, as he now liked to dub her, would act as an able, if semi-official, co-regent. None could compete with her wisdom and ready wit, qualities already tested during his first Syrian expeditions and much envied by the two Great Royal Wives, Nefertari and Isisnofret.

The queen mother, Mut-Tuya. Egyptian Museum, Cairo.

Towards the temples of the south

R AMSES, THEN, WAS TO TRAVEL to the lands of the south, renewing direct contact with provincial dignitaries, to whom the tale of Kadesh would be told, for none should be in any doubt as to his extraordinary prowess. Pharaoh was, moreover, desirous to establish closer ties with his subjects. From the very start of his reign he had also cherished plans for major works; on these he focused great attention, since he did not intend simply to apply the traditional program. More than ever, the temple, in its very structure and décor, was to refer to the great moments of history, as well as conveying more effectively than hitherto the cosmic forces on whose balance the world depends.

First of all, it was necessary, on all buildings erected to the glory of the multiple aspects of the demiurge, to perpetuate the miraculous and gigantic battle he had fought, practically alone, against the most powerful of his adversaries from the north and east. The magic effects ensuing from these reliefs would then guarantee his invincibility in all future actions.

The tri-unity after Amenophis IV-Akhenaten

To summarize the core concept of a religious teaching, such as Ramses intended to disseminate it, it is as well to refer briefly to a number of terms in a text contemporary with the post-Amarna period and the beginning of the Nineteenth Dynasty, contained in a papyrus currently held at Leiden (I -350). A testimony to the syncretism of the time, it refers to the tri-unity of Amun-Re-Ptah—three godheads possessed of a single will. This is the passage from Chapter 300 of this hymn to Amun:

All the gods are three: Amun-Re-Ptah! None are like unto them. Hidden is the name [the principle] *in the quality of Amun; the face is Re; the body, Ptah. Their cities on earth are established forever: Thebes, Heliopolis, and Memphis, for all eternity. . . .*
For all, the life or death depends on him. . . . Amun, Re [and Ptah], all three together.

Statue of the creator god Ptah, seated. Egyptian sculpture, New Kingdom, Eighteenth Dynasty. Museo Egiziano, Turin.

As one would expect, the text is hardly crystal clear; the only salient fact is that the dogma of tri-unity is so underlined as to appear unimpeachable.

The return of Seth

RAMSES' INTENTION WAS TO JOIN to this trinity the image of Seth. Seti had placed him at the head of the fourth division of his army; Ramses was counting on the actions of the Seth division emanating from his new capital, Pi-Ramesse-the-Victorious, where the impact of its oldest temple, at the south of the city, was seconded by sanctuaries to Amun, Re, and Ptah at the three other cardinal points of the metropolis.

The concept of Amun (*Imen*, the "concealed"), now the object of much comment, was gradually taking over the other divine forms. For instance, it is Amun-Atum who is busy inscribing the name of the sovereign on the fruits of the *ished* tree; there was an Amun-Min, master of the fertile warmth of the earth, and an Amun-Nile enthroned on a dais made of the flood waters. Amun's ram's horn on the side of Pharaoh's face meanwhile sought to demonstrate his earthly deification.

At the most fraught moment of his existence, had not Amun answered Ramses' appeal before the citadel of Kadesh? By enriching the realm occupied by the tri-unity, Ramses strengthened the universalist spirit of his program and minimized the power base of

The god Amun (Amun-Min). Temple of Thutmosis III, Deir el-Bahri.

any single clergy. Amun could thus overlay the influence of various theologies: each recognized in him "his" god—and principally those who had no access to the temples. He appeared as something like a "God of the Downtrodden," as B. Gunn nicely put it. These were the people Ramses was intent on promoting, later recommending his High Priest Bakenkhons to allow space on the east front in the great temple at Karnak to allow the faithful access to "Amun-who-listens-to-prayers."

The architectural program

R AMSES WAS AWARE THAT IT would take two full cycles of the Inundation for the reforms designed to "modernize" his army to enter into effect: only then would he be able to muster his forces and retake the lost terrain. He thus had ample time to realize something else particularly dear to his heart: to give concrete form to his program of architectural symbolism.

Ram of Amun. Temple of Amun, Luxor.

Before he reached the domain of Amun, he had stopped at Abydos near another temple on the brink of completion. There he ordered that the Bulletin of the battle be reproduced on the outer walls to the north and west.

Once in the region of Thebes, the atmosphere would have reminded the king of his youth, when, attended by Paser, he visited the construction sites on the left bank, and of his time at Karnak during the "investiture" of the high priest of Amun, Nebwennef. Since that time, moreover, his consecration had transformed him definitively into the son of the god, while he was increasingly characterizing himself as the Hero of Kadesh.

In the "House" of Amun, he chose to have evocative scenes from the Bulletin (later replaced by other battle episodes) carved on the south-facing outer wall of the hypostyle, as well as along the south-western accesses to the temple. At Luxor, he made a point of portraying the principal phases of the Bulletin on the outside of the courtyards and on the northern face of the pylon towers no fewer than three times, thereby affording the public ample opportunity to admire them.

The favorite temple: the Ramesseum

F INALLY, AFTER CROSSING THE RIVER, he could spend some time in his beloved Temple of a Million Years, the Ramesseum so named by Champollion, but which in the late classical period, when Diodorus Siculus visited Egypt, was believed to be the tomb of Ozymandias. Building work was almost complete, but the decoration remained in abeyance. All around, the domain featured storerooms in which the temple treasury accumulated: on the northern, western, and southern flanks, immense attics with arched roofs were filled with grain reserves to pay the necropolis's priests and workmen, together with materials to adorn the temple furniture and other elements of the cult, as well as a great mass of gifts offered to the crown on the New Year's Day. To these were added dwellings for the priests, administrative offices, laboratories, the library, and the House of Life, including a vast scriptorium.* The southwestern corner was reserved for an open-air workshop in which the sacred vases and statues were fashioned and carved.

Lastly, the southeastern corner was the site of the small palace for the monarch, where he might be received when he came to undergo the annual rite of regeneration. The enclosure was to be delimited on three sides—north, west and south—by a double avenue of sphinxes: to the west, these had human heads and protected a statuette of the pharaoh standing between their legs; those to the north and the south had animal heads.

Scriptorium: workshop in which copyists wrote out their manuscripts.

The Ramesseum, consecrated to the god Amun. Thebes.

*The Ramesseum;
the stores in
the economic zone.*

Instead of the traditional single courtyard, the first zone of the temple contained a pair. The second zone was dedicated primarily to the hypostyle hall, while the third featured a suite of rooms surrounding the inner sanctum. For representations of the battle of Kadesh, Ramses chose the lower register of the eastern wall in the second court; he demanded that work on the decoration of the western interior wall of the pylon be postponed because, alongside a new portrayal of Kadesh, that space was to be reserved for a carving of his future campaigns to Canaan and Amurru.

Ramses takes inspiration from the innovations of Amenophis IV–Akhenaten

One of the reasons Ramses had come to Thebes was the keen attraction he felt, even in his young days, for the Amarna period. As we have seen, it was a multifaceted phenomenon, and it had a number of consequences on the interpretation given to the image of Amun. Above and beyond this, however, there was the dogma of Osiris that governed all the funerary rites and which had gradually become more accessible to the Egyptian populace, and the mystery of which governed the customs of the faithful.

Ramses was persuaded that the divine concept of the Aten, the solar disk, had not been invented by Amenophis IV but had been latent in Egypt since the dawn of time. He was also well aware that the various forms of the divine that from time immemorial had filled the temples were designed to activate a growing consciousness of the infinite variety of the creative power among the common people.

Osiris, as envisaged by Amenophis IV–Akhenaten

In short, Ramses had well and truly grasped what Akhenaten had had to contend with. It is hard to believe that the reforming pharaoh had rejected the myth of Osiris when he had had himself depicted in the attitude of the divinity, his legs together (and thus static), his arms crossed over his chest, and with his hands grasping the regalia of the god, the crook and flail? At the beginning of his "heresy," he had even deployed these on the "Osirid pillars" of the great Temple of Aten to the east of Karnak. And had he not also had his funerary furniture—coffin and sarcophagus—prepared so as to receive the "Osirian" mummy complete with the requisite funerary statuettes, the *sh abti* (or *shawbti*), so typical of the traditional rites, whose first object had been the martyr god, Osiris himself. There were not, then, two fundamental and mutually incompatible truths, one striving unceasingly to delve deeper into the secrets of the vital force, the other probing the mysteries of death: these were merely two faces of a single, seamless phenomenon. Life and death cannot function without one another; they are complementary, and together incorporate all the manifestations of the divine.

Patently Amenophis IV-Akhenaten's desire was to gloss a reality whose incomparable grandeur resides in simplicity. He hoped to clarify a certain ambiguity, a state of ignorance supported by myths which, though framed to render the all-encompassing laws of nature more comprehensible, often ended up by obscuring them.

Akhenaten in the pose of the god Osiris. Egyptian Museum, Cairo.

The Osiride pillars

In the temples, the famous Osiride pillars, rectangular pillars at the front of which is a statue of the king ensconced in the funerary sheath of Osiris, had appeared as early as the Middle Kingdom. The statue of the king was frozen in the attitude of the mummified dead god, but standing, and holding the scepters of Osiris.

To bring out the full significance of this image in connection with the jubilee ceremonies of New Year's Day, held in the Temples of a Million Years, it had to be shown to be the symbol of dormant forces from which "new vigor would surge forth." This is what Akhenaten attempted.

Akhenaten's "reform" as understood by Ramses

This bold reform, translated even into architecture, could not have left Ramses indifferent. In laying out the Ramesseum on the left bank of Thebes, in consultation with those in whom he had the greatest confidence—Nebwennef, high priest of Karnak; Wennofer, high priest of Osiris at Abydos; and the foremost scholar of the region, the scribe Ramose, close to the vizier Paser—Ramses tried to come up with a means of reframing this brilliant demonstration of the rites of regeneration more discreetly, so as to avoid shocking the clergy. He thus added a second court to the plan initially envisaged for his temple: the first was to be bordered by a peristyle* decorated with traditional Osiride pillars evoking the sovereign's state at the beginning of the ceremony of regeneration (that is, wrapped in the shroud); the other courtyard, similarly designed architecturally, was also encircled by pillars, but against these the effigy of the king, his feet still joined, was dressed in the royal apron (*shendot*) of the living and wore the solar headdress. These images of the revivified king were flanked by statuettes of the royal children. When, after his barge moored at the temple quay, Ramses passed through the great gate of the Pylon of the Ramesseum and caught sight of these "solarized" effigies, which the crowd would be able to admire on leaving the sanctuary, his satisfaction knew no bounds. Having gazed on the immense colossus abutting the southern jamb of the door at the rear of the court and noted the preparations for the erection of the great statue to the north, he would have then moved into the second courtyard, where, before proceeding to the large hall with its papyrus columns, he would have seen the royal mummiform image standing before each pillar; just like the previous ones (and those of Abu Simbel later), each of these statues measured sixteen cubits, the height of the ideal Nile Flood.

Here, more than ever, statuary played an integral part in the meaning and efficacity of the rite of Pharaoh's procession at the New Year festival. It is made clear that the Egyptian temple must reflect on earth the image of the world in which the demiurge has placed man: the dwelling of the god, laid on the primeval mound, had to materialize concepts of the broadest nature.

The central symbol of the hypostyle

Each return of the Flood marked the beginning of a New Year comprised of three seasons of four months each. The cycle, for whose regular recurrence Egyptians prayed so ardently, had for millennia been divided into twelve thirty-day months (plus five and a quarter additional days), forming, on the basis of three "weeks" of ten days each, the thirty-six *decans* of the three seasons. The imperative was, by all possible means, to incite, encourage, and plead for the cycle of the months to return and for the year to end without fail with the long-awaited reappearance of the nourishing Flood.

Peristyle: gallery of columns surround a building within its enclosing wall, and thus distinct from a colonnade.

Pages 96–97:
Second peristyle court at the Ramesseum, set with Osirid pillars. Thebes-West.

The hypostyle hall and its columns with campaniform capitals at the Ramesseum. Thebes-West.

Ramses, then, intended his hypostyle to form the framework for a complete cycle, with the twelve months materialized by twelve papyrus columns with blossoming capitals. The king appeared in majesty on the side of each of these columns, making offerings to a divine form. He was escorted by the image of his *ka*, a genius evoking his divine potential, bearing on his head the "banner" containing the Horus name of Pharaoh.

The twelve columns were flanked on both sides, to east and west, by eighteen smaller, similar papyrus columns, but with closed capitals. In this manner the year was escorted by its thirty-six *decans*. This solar circuit was meant to culminate naturally in the materialization of New Year's Day as represented in the following room.

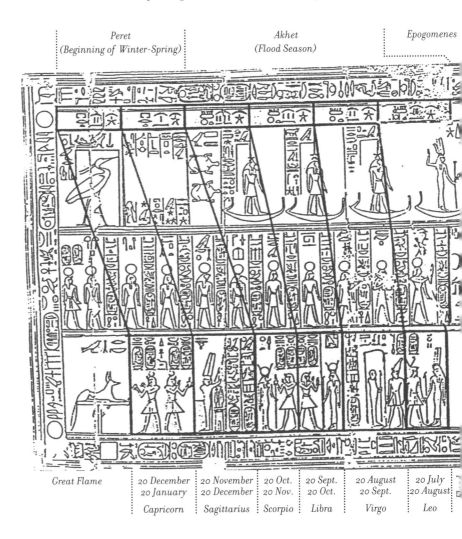

	Peret (Beginning of Winter-Spring)		Akhet (Flood Season)			Epogomenes

| Great Flame | 20 December 20 January Capricorn | 20 November 20 December Sagittarius | 20 Oct. 20 Nov. Scorpio | 20 Sept. 20 Oct. Libra | 20 August 20 Sept. Virgo | 20 July 20 August Leo |

The astronomy room

A large corniced door dominated by a long frieze of *neheb* signs evoking the eternity of the sun and facing the central colonnade led from the hypostyle to a rectangular hall ornamented with eight columns with closed papyrus capitals. The reason it is called the "astronomy room" is because part of the ceiling borne by the four columns to the north is decorated with symbols of the constellations and dominated by a linear calendar.

The calendar

The instructions of Ramses were incontrovertible: the calendar was to be laid out in such a way that the sign for the New Year would

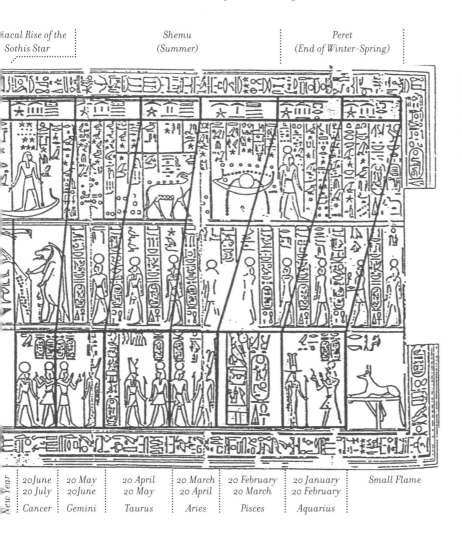

Drawing of the astronomical ceiling in the Ramesseum. The diagonal lines connect indications of the months of the year (top) with the corresponding dates (lower register).

	Heliacal Rise of the Sothis Star			Shemu (Summer)				Peret (End of Winter-Spring)	

New Year	20 June 20 July	20 May 20 June	20 April 20 May	20 March 20 April	20 February 20 March	20 January 20 February	Small Flame
	Cancer	Gemini	Taurus	Aries	Pisces	Aquarius	

occupy the middle of the ceiling. This day marked the beginning of the first season, *akhet*, formed by the four months during which the Flood covered all the arable land of that year, up to the sands of the Libyan and Arabian deserts. Then came the second season, *peret* (winter–spring), four months during which the farmer had time to prepare the soil (which, thanks to the waters, was rich in new alluvia), to sow, and to begin reaping. The third part of the year was constituted by *shemu*, during which the harvest had to be completed before the onset of the hot season, which brought all kinds of fearsome troubles in its wake, but ended with the joys of grape-picking and the advent of the New Year.

Just below this, the New Year's axis is framed by the image of Orion and Sothis, the miraculous star that reappears on the eastern horizon at dawn after remaining unseen for seventy days. Immediately after this, the rising sun emerges at its side. The heliacal rising of the star Sothis (around July 18) was followed shortly afterwards by the onset of the Flood. The base of the ceiling depicted the cynocephalus* of Thoth, the master of time, sitting face-forward on the *djed* pillar and gazing south.

Cynocephalus: African monkey whose head resembles that of a dog.

New Year's Day

It so happens that the long-desired Flood announced by the star of Sothis arrives from the south, so this new scientific-symbolic image also marks Ramses' commitment to perpetuating such teachings in his temple. The building was governed by a sort of celestial mechanics, the cogs and wheels of which were positioned with the utmost care: the twelve months, the three seasons, the thirty-six *decans* all vibrate in the solar sandstone out of which the sanctuary was constructed. The walls of the astronomy room bore, *inter alia*, the image of the *ished* tree, designed to bring about the perpetual cycle of renovation, since its energies, rooted in the god, underwrote the continued life of the country.

A bas-relief on the eastern wall of the astronomy room also depicted the procession of boats of the royal genius, of the saint of the royal necropolis (Ahmes-Nefertari), of the Thebes triad (Amun-Mut-Khonsu), and of Imenet. Above all, Ramses was determined to underline that this New Year's Day marked the return of the divine flood that contains within it all hope of life, and through which "Amun-the-hidden," twinned with Re-Horakhty, found expression.

A stone clock

Among the astronomical symbols, the twenty-four hours of the apparent solar revolution were sure not to escape royal consideration, and proposals were made to mention them in the three successive eight-columned rooms of the Holy of Holies, built in to prolong the axis of the hypostyle hall. It should not be forgotten that these buildings were chiefly reserved for the ritual confirmation of royal power, celebrated each year, and not just in daylight but also at night—during which the king reposed on a ceremonial litter—which constituted the ultimate backdrop to Pharaoh's cyclical regeneration.

The Holy of Holies and royal rejuvenation

To the south of the Holy of Holies, Ramses had made a point of placing buildings in which ritual stopping-places associated him with the various phases of Nature, so that he might provide for his country through acts of "sympathetic magic." A bas-relief in the Osiris rooms located to the southwest showed him reliving the three seasons of the Osiris year. He starts by taking up the plough, a gesture which should be seen as exemplifying Pharaoh's responsibility to ensure widespread agriculture. He is then seen reaping with a sickle and thereby materializing a successful harvest. Later, after the hot season, New Year's Day arrives, symbolized by the image of *Hapy*, the Flood: Ramses offers up prayers to ensure that the four months of "manna" are spread over the whole country and bring about the rebirth of the natural world. On the opposite side, to the northeast, the "solar" rooms were intended to sanction the annual revival, the guarantor of continuance in all its forms, the goal on which all the rites converged.

Ramses (III) performing ritual "agricultural labor" in the Osirid hall of his Jubilee Temple.

Amun protects Ramses

There were still many other topics left to treat in this "House of a Million Years," which Ramses was to share with "Amun-the-hidden." Had not the god ridden roughshod over every obstacle and afforded him supernatural protection? In consequence, the southwest wall of the hypostyle was dedicated to a sumptuous decoration showing Pharaoh receiving the victorious *harpe* from the hands of the lord of Karnak enthroned in majesty and

Ramses receives the khepesh *of victory from Amun. Hypostyle hall, Ramesseum.*

accompanied by his divine consort, Mut. Priority, naturally, was granted to scenes from the battle of Kadesh that Pharaoh had carved beneath the northeast portico in the second court, against the western face of the First Pylon. But it should also be pointed out that he ordered his decorators to wait for the campaigns he was planning in Canaan and Amurru, so as to illustrate a future triumph he trusted would prove complete.

The introduction of the family

By the end of his thirtieth year, the king's family already boasted a good many offspring. After Abu Simbel, these new additions were to appear again in the temple: a double register to either side of the door of the hypostyle room leading to the astronomical hall had already been devoted, in the north, to the procession of his daughters and, in the south, to a regularly updated list of the princes. In addition, each of the names of his respective sons, carved in vertical columns, was accompanied by a column that was left empty, destined to receive complementary inscriptions pertaining to the princes as they grew up. Thus we see that, after the sixty-seventh year of Ramses' reign, the thirteenth name, that of young prince Merenptah, was updated with an indication of the titles and throne name of the new monarch, who had already outlived a number of his brothers.

The craftsmen of the Ramesseum

The time had come to reward with gifts of gold and silver the chief builder, Penre, the head of the security forces, the *Medjay*, who had toiled in the Ramesseum from the time the foundations had been laid, the architect Imeneminet and his assistants the head foremen, and all the trade associations for their remarkably skilled work: already the temple bore a polychrome décor on a white ground, the purpose of which, as in all Egyptian religious buildings, was to bring the reliefs and sculptures in the round to life. It was also important not to forget all those Egyptian—and, of course, foreign—laborers who had provided the manpower.

In addition, Ramses was to make a speech to the head of the *Medjay*, Hatia, whose father had erected the enormous statues of the Ramesseum and doubtless helped to install the largest of the colossi, to the south of the Second Pylon. A little later, he must have also erected the flagpoles in front of the temple of Amun. Eager as he was to concern himself with the fate of all those who had served him, Ramses was also keen to thank another Medjay chief, Iuny, "valorous officer responsible for ensuring order in the country," who must have done much to assist in the construction of the hypostyle hall.

Ramses was flanked by Tia, whom he had appointed as overseer of the treasury and of cattle at the Ramesseum at his crowning. Tia, his sister's husband, was a stalwart, but Ramses had no hesitation in enrolling men of foreign origin (other than Nubian) in positions of trust to administer the Ramesseum, one such being Ramessesemperre. In reality, this Canaanite, originally from Zin-Bashan, after his arrival under the name Ben-Azen as part of the spoils of war, had probably been raised at the *kep* school, near the palace or the harem. He had risen to become one of the most trusted servants of Pharaoh. Later, another civil servant, likewise of foreign origin, became chief overseer of the Ramesseum: Yupa, son of General Urhiya, succeeding his father in the post.

Ramses' hidden agenda

Dᴜʀɪɴɢ ʜɪs sᴏᴊᴏᴜʀɴ ᴏɴ the left bank of Thebes, Ramses had realized that, though most of the temple buildings had been made out of sandstone blocks extracted from the quarries of Gebel Silsileh, replaced by alabaster and black or pink granite elements wherever symbolism demanded, the Medjay chiefs had not hesitated to remove from the nearby Jubilee Temples of the Eighteenth

Dynasty materials nearer to hand. If Ramses had indeed been informed of these "borrowings" from the sanctuary of Queen Hatshepsut in Deir el-Bahri (*Djeser djeseru*), would he not bear a measure of responsibility for the systematic obliteration and destruction that damaged it so grievously?

Close examination of the great procession of royal ancestors presented by Ramses both in the Temple of Abydos and in the Ramesseum supplies an answer. In the latter temple, the presentation of the statuettes of the supposed ancestors of the monarch borne in by priests does indeed include—where the kings of the New Kingdom are concerned—effigies of all those who reigned up to the time of Ramses, with the exception of Hatshepsut and the protagonists of the Amarna period: Amenophis IV-Akhenaten, Smenkhkara, Ay, and Tutankhamun. The list is resumed with Horemheb.

How can such omissions be explained? Surely because a sop had to be offered to the clergies of Amun and Osiris. The initiatives of Hatshepsut and Amenophis IV had inspired Ramses; he wanted to have them adopted, but he had to "disguise" them and mask his sources; in consequence, he saw it as his duty to ostensibly reject their creators. This makes it easier to appreciate why the monument of Deir el-Bahri and the city of Akhetaten were destroyed during his reign.

The *mammisi** of the king at Thebes

The queen mother

ONE CONCERN WAS EVER-PRESENT in Pharaoh's mind: the veneration and gratitude to which he unceasingly testified with regard to his mother Tuya. Before becoming queen and embracing her royal duties by the side of a valiant prince, this noble lady from a military and aristocratic caste had already enjoyed an active life. In her youth, she had on occasion had to stand by him, and was thus better prepared than the royal princesses to assume her responsibilities when Seti, crowned Pharaoh, was in the wars in Syria or in "the wretched land of Kush." Since her son had ascended to the throne, she had assisted him, just as she had her husband formerly: ever since his return from Kadesh, Ramses had remained greatly impressed by her actions. For this reason, she had been able to play the role of unofficial co-regent for more than ten years, while her son was away, most of the time making war.

On the death of Seti, Ramses ordered work to be resumed on the edifice on the left bank of Thebes, which was to be further enlarged.

Mammisi:
certain buildings linked to the Egyptian temples, sometimes thought to be "birth houses" celebrating the births of the gods.

Ramses II and his mother,
Tuya. Kunsthistorisches
Museum, Vienna.

Not only was the temple to be dedicated to his mother, but it would also feature elements for Nefertari and for the "troop" of his children, as testified by vestiges discovered in the surrounding area. It was also Ramses's intention to devote the temple to the myth of the royal birth, designed to obscure the fact that, at the time Lady Tuya had brought him into the world, she could not possibly have been visited by Amun the procreator: it was necessary, therefore, to restage the event and, through the mysteries of theogamy, transform him into a child fathered by the god.

Theogamy

Since the time of the pyramids, in the absence of reliefs from temples that have since vanished, literary allusions had elucidated the notion of theogamy, an act by which the god replaced Pharaoh at the time of the royal *hymen*, making the child about to be brought into the world the son of the god. Only the fertilizing divine spirit was able to change its appearance. In the Fifth Dynasty, it came in the form of Re. In the New Kingdom, the progenitor took the material shape of Amun. Thus, Pharaoh Hatshepsut, daughter of Tuthmosis I and Queen Ahmose, was sired by the master of Thebes. In spite of the hammer blows, one can still see, under the northern colonnade of the temple at Deir el-Bahri, a series of reliefs illustrating the principle stages of the miracle: the hymen, followed by the

a: Thoth's "annunciation"
to the queen.
b: Khnum fashioning the
divine child with his ka
on his potter's wheel.
c: The queen conducted
to the birthing-room.
d: After the queen has
given birth, nurses feed
both the child and his ka.
e: The divine child and
his ka presented to their
progenitor Amun.

"annunciation" of the miracle to the queen, the birth of the divinely
incarnate child and his *ka*, and finally the presentation of the newborn to his illustrious forebear.

An analogous scene is preserved at the Temple of Luxor, where
a room is given over to the congress of Amun with Mutemwia,
mother of the future Amenophis III, the builder of the sanctuary.
Up to this period, only one space in the same temple had been put
aside for the evocation of the divine exploit that sanctifies the
unearthly origin of Pharaoh. All occurred in the secrecy of the
sanctuary. It is here that Seti (probably) and Ramses (certainly)
broke with tradition. The aim in removing the room of the
theogamy from the main building was to magnify the event and
incorporate it into a sanctuary of its own. By giving it an importance and autonomy visible to all, and by adding further buildings
to the sanctuary, the radiance of the divine could be extended to
the family and to all the descendants represented in the reliefs.

Ramses, then, must also be credited with having ordained the creation of a new type of sanctuary—in the form of a chapel for the birth of Horus-son-of-Isis (conflated with Pharaoh)—formerly believed to have arisen only in the Greco-Roman era. The first *mammisi* had existed under Ramses, therefore, and referred to his miraculous birth. Ramses laid down the plans for his "House of a Million Years" in such a way that his *mammisi* abuts the hypostyle hall to the north, a discovery I was privileged to make in 1970, while supervising research on the site.

Dedication of Ramses to his mother. Mammisi, Ramesseum, Thebes.

How to reconstitute a vanished monument

On the leveled zones of the monument, on which only a few column bases remain, together with traces of a number of walls on the ground, I located a stone which, stuck in rubble from an approach ramp, bore the inscription: "He made this monument for his mother. . . ." Several years later, a fragment from a Hathor capital indicated the style of the monument, which was devoted to a female entity. Vestiges of the names of Ramses and Nefertari then enabled me to make further progress in my investigation. Now all I had to do was to consult those architectural elements bearing representations linked to scenes of Ramesside theogamy that had been reemployed in a later building not far from there, at Medinet Habu, on blocks from the ceiling bearing foundation texts for the queen mother, *Mut*-Tuya. Finally, a doorframe was made of pieces from a Hathor capital dominated by the names of Ramses and *Mut*-Tuya. The scattered ruins still bore the name of the principal beneficiary, *Mut*-Tuya, followed by that of Nefertari, and those of the children of the son of the god who was shortly to be deified on earth.

Fragment of Hathor capital. Mammisi, Ramesseum, Thebes.

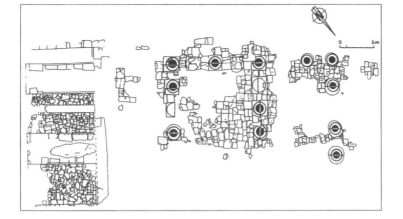

Drawings of the vestiges on the ground in the mammisi. *Ramesseum, Thebes.*

The promotion of the queen mother

The *mammisi*, then, now an independent monument to the glory of the union between Amun and *Mut*-Tuya, was also Ramses' creation, if undoubtedly influenced by his unspoken inspirer, Akhenaten. In this respect too, Ramses outdid his predecessor. The early sovereigns certainly gloried in divine parenthood; none, however, had ever asserted or claimed divine essence for their mother. It is this experiment that Ramses seems to have attempted. He often affixed the name *Mut*, divine consort of Amun, to the initial name of his mother. Even while the queen was still living, occurrences of *Mut*-Tuya were frequent, and the name of the goddess was even familiarly used in coining the diminutive *Muty*. All these subtleties of expression betray how determined Ramses was to obfuscate not only his civil but even his human origins!

Reconstituted elevation of the frontage of Ramses' mammisi, *parallel to that of the hypostyle hall of the Great Temple.*

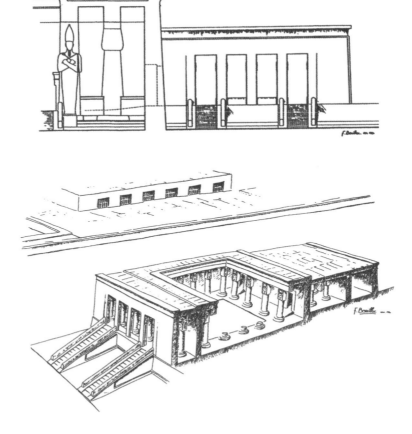

Axonometric section of the mammisi.

Queen dowager and Great Royal Wife

At the rear of the small temple, two chapels had been reserved for the two *grandes dames* of the beginning of the reign: the queen mother, *Mut*-Tuya, and the Great Royal Wife, Nefertari, mother of the crown prince. As a transition between the "House of a Million Years" and the *mammisi*, the images of the two queens were represented at the entrance to the hypostyle, both playing the sistrum-*naos** and heading towards the small temple dedicated to them. Both sport the large upright plume on their head. In one of their cases, only the feathers are visible: we are in the presence of the dowager, whose fecundity has waned. On the other hand, the headdress on the figure of Nefertari, who proceeds first, also sports the high tapering horns framing a solar sphere: this is the standard ornament of Sothis, the star which annually regenerates both the year itself and the sovereign.

Sistrum-*naos*: a *sistrum* resembles a rattle; the *naos* is the "Holy of Holies," the inner sanctum containing a statuette in the image of the god or goddess.

Progress on the Ramesseum was proceeding at the desired pace, and Pharaoh promised himself he would return to Thebes to see how things were getting on after the future Syrian campaign. Countless reliefs recorded new episodes in the royal epic. The final touch to the *mammisi* would be the construction of two approach ramps to the terrace that cannot date to earlier than the eighth year of his reign.

Towards a new message in architecture

Before regaining his radiant northern capital, Ramses had to take the road to the province of Nubia so as to pursue his schemes for building sanctuaries dedicated to the various entities protecting his empire on which the annual manifestation of *hapy*, the life-giving Flood, depended.

Ramses and the plans for Nubian temples

Leaving Heliopolis in the south, Ramses sailed back up the river on his royal vessel. When the two banks began to narrow at Gebel Silsileh, where in the early years of his reign he had had erected a large stele to the honor of *Hapy*, Ramses knew he was nearing the First Cataract.

Aswan

This was truly the gateway to Africa. For all time, Syene, which we today call Aswan, was the site of the largest market in the entire continent. The most diverse ethnic groups rubbed shoulders, exchanging produce of an incredible variety that arrived there from the southernmost regions. Considerable quantities of gold, extracted from the mines of Nubia, and most of the time treated on the spot, transited through the valley, under the supervision of the provincial governor. Various warehouses regularly delivered north goods that tribute—or barter—had stockpiled in vast stores controlled by the viceroys of Wawat and Kush (i.e. Lower and Upper Nubia, the latter being modern-day Sudan), responsible for maintaining order and collecting annual taxes in kind. People would also look on admiringly at the constant stream of wild animal skins, ostrich eggs and feathers, elephant tusks, semi-precious stones and beasts for His Majesty's exotic garden: guenons, sacred baboons, cheetahs, panthers, lions, giraffes... Last but not least, the Nubians were past masters in ship-building, and countless boats from the yards not far from Kuban would call at Aswan before continuing on to the metropolis.

The arrival of Nefertari

In the blazing, arid climate, where enormous boulders of pink granite eroded black must have looked like herds of elephants at the water's edge, the view that offered itself to Nefertari, now that her ship had joined that of the king, must have been a truly memorable one. The island of Abu, which the Greeks dubbed Elephantine, was inhabited by the local dignitaries, whose flower-covered residences encircled the temple where local images of the divinity were worshipped: Satet (Satis) and Anket (Anuket) surrounded by ram-headed Khnum, the "African," who with silt and water from the cataract had fashioned humanity on his potter's wheel. The citadel, once so necessary under the Middle Kingdom, still existed, but had by now almost lost its purpose.

The land of Wawat

The gifts presented to the royal couple came in a ceaseless flow, but they would soon have to weigh anchor, making the most of the Nile's high water to cross the First Cataract and make headway down the route ordained by Pharaoh, following an itinerary planned by the viceroy of Nubia, Iuny. The first leg of the journey upriver was to end at the outstream of Wadi Allaki on the right bank. This led to the gold-mines close to the town of Baki (Kuban), where the king had erected the famous stele for the well dug for the miners, and where the massive fortress of the Middle Kingdom still towered.

The hemispeos of Gerf Hussein

The northern zone of the land of Wawat was now chosen by Ramses as the site of a future *hemispeos* to be dug out in honor of the god

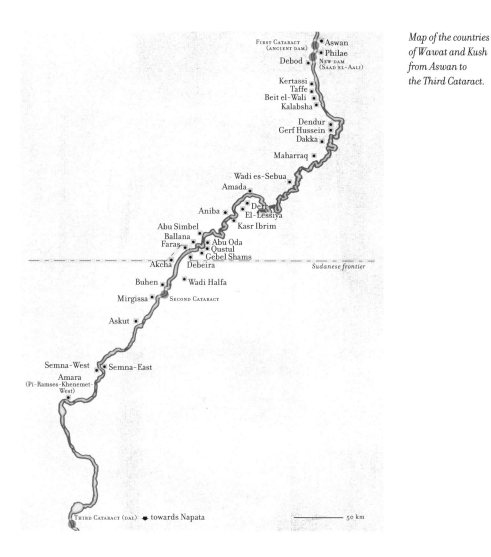

Map of the countries of Wawat and Kush from Aswan to the Third Cataract.

Ptah: in our time the place would become known under the name of Gerf Hussein. A pale reflection of Abu Simbel, the decoration was surely the work of local craftsmen.

Speos *and* hemispeos

The great temples of the delta and Thebes were built on stone foundations and were preceded by imposing pylons whose mythological and symbolic function was to bring forth the morning sun. The three zones of the divine dwelling-place (excluding the court) were roofed over with ceilings that formed terraces. Comprising the temple itself and outbuildings, the complex was surrounded by high walls of sun-dried brick, making it look somewhat like a bastion. The divine House was above all designed for the maintenance of the "cosmic machine," and to this end was staffed by a specialized and hierarchically organized personnel, including servants, aided and abetted by scholars from every discipline. It was, however, totally closed to the populace.

Ramses was cognizant of the architectural innovation introduced by Hatshepsut into her monument at Deir el-Bahri, with its stepped temple, the top terrace of which gave onto shrines dug out of the mountainside against which the building rose. Similarly, the rock-cut temple in Middle Egypt, the *Speos* Artemidos, was an invention of Hatshepsut's.

On the Nubian riverbanks, Ramses erected altars of repose for the divine vehicle that borrowed their appearance from the *speos* (cave) or *hemispeos* dedicated to the four divine entities. The sanctuaries at Pi-Ramesse surveyed the four points of the compass, and it should be recalled that at the end of his co-regency Ramses had already laid out the small sanctuary of Beit el-Wali in the style of a *hemispeos*.

As will be seen, the four original foundations planned by Ramses in Nubia were to present close ties with the phenomenon of the Flood and constituted the most visible demonstration of how the king's life was intimately bound up with the forces on which Egypt depended. Though he was confident in the effectiveness of his program, in no way did he mean it to evince the cult of the sun's action as established and materialized from earlier times in the four Horus of Nubia: the Horus of *Baki* (Kuban), the Horus of *Miam* (Aniba), the Horus of *Meha* (Abu Simbel), and the Horus of *Buhen* (Wadi Halfa), near the Second Cataract. For this reason, Ramses one day had part of the sanctuary dedicated to Ptah, sixty miles (a hundred kilometers) to the south of Aswan, dug out into a cave. At the front, a court embellished with Osirid pillars with the figure of the king in "living" costume recalled those in the Ramesseum.

Nubian landscapes

Trail: ornamental motif, often mural, composed of a continuous band of flowering stems looping over vases, mascarons, and small figures arranged within the scrollwork.

The further south the procession pushed, the greener the Nubian landscape became. Date-palms, dum-palms, and sweet-smelling wild mimosa covered the banks. Women and children ran towards the river to admire the cortège of royal boats, the sails of which were adorned with geometric and trail* patterns woven in colored thread; the barges were escorted by those of the viceroy of Nubia and the official guard.

Converts to Egyptian civilization, the Nubians kept faith with their roots and their traditions. Back in their own land, they were all buried in the Nubian style, simply wrapped in a goatskin. Only the very occasional member of the élite made a point of being interred in the Egyptian manner, in a vault-cum-chapel hewn out of the rock. One such was a certain Hekanefer, son of a Nubian chief, raised in the palace school (the *kep*) and a classmate of Tutankhamun's, who had returned to take up the post of governor to his native Nubia in the area round Aniba, the capital at that time.

The Wadi es-Sebua

The boats made a halt where caravans from the western Libyan desert alighted. In the years to come, the site would present the requisite conditions for a large temple dedicated to the power of Amun, whom travelers to every destination would pray to in the guise of "Amun of the Ways." This sanctuary, another *hemispeos*, "saved from the waters" like the majority of Nubian temples, today bears the name of Wadi es-Sebua, "the Valley of the Lions," because of the sphinxes composing its *dromos*.*

Dromos: avenue bordered by sphinxes that extends outside, along the axis of a temple connecting it with another building or a landing-stage on the Nile.

Temple of Wadi-Sebua, partial view of the avenue of the sphinxes (with falcon heads in the second court, and with human heads in the first court). Nubia.

Waystations for the barque

The "spark" had been lit at Amada. The message conveyed by the sanctuaries that Ramses intended to consecrate on the banks of Nubia had recently been given final form: the four main sanctuaries with which Ramses was to endow Nubia would be immense wayside altars for the divine barque of Amun-Re, symbolizing the arrival of the Flood as it crosses the Second Cataract on its life-giving journey to Egypt. But there would also be the two mounds of *Ibshek* and *Meha* (Abu Simbel) to reveal the mystery of New Year's Day, ensuring its regular recurrence and associating the actions of the royal couple with the phenomenon that bestowed life on their kingdom.

Before leaving Amada, Ramses had given orders to restore the reliefs of the temple built and decorated under the kings Tuthmosis III, Amenophis II, and Tuthmosis IV, where the images of Amun had been zealously obliterated by the acolytes of the disk of Aten at the time of Amenophis IV–Akhenaten. The coarseness of the restoration work, still visible today, testifies to a hastily executed job, entrusted to craftsmen with little interest in aesthetics: the main thing had been to offer fresh and tangible assurances to the clergy of Amun.

The land of the "Golden One"

Nefertari must have been dazzled by the splendor of the countryside between Amada and Miam. The luminous air of Nubia, far from the dusty soil raised by the spring winds, seemed encapsulated in pure crystal. As the hours and days drifted by, Nefertari's vessel advanced along a river ploughed into furrows of turquoise, amethyst, or peridot. As the brief twilight fell, the sky and waters fused together into gold, sliced through by a piercing blade of light thrown out by the dying sun. The queen understood why when people spoke of this region they also always mentioned gold. The deposits were rich, of course, but even the very sand seemed soaked in it. These regions, haunted by the legend of distant lands, of Hathor with her many faces—of death, but also of love which gives back life—had lent one of their names to the goddess: Hathor was indeed the Golden One, the *Nubet*.

Miam and Toshke

The arable land on the left bank of the Nile widened still farther: the flotilla was about come to the region around Wawat's capital, the city of Miam. Recently, Ramses had given orders to transfer his administrative stronghold further south, into the country of Kush. This new residence had also been named Pi-Ramesse. The idea was to stress an official Egyptian presence in the areas of northern Sudan, in the ancient countries of *Iam*, populated by warriors little inclined to embrace the more urbane manners of their conquerors. They were about to go beyond the zone of Toshke—since the Old Kingdom, yet another terminus for caravans from Aswan crossing the sands on their asses from oasis to oasis. The region was renowned for its famous quarries of diorite and jaspers.

El-Lessiya

On the right bank, the rocks gained in relief: the sovereigns had traveled past the caves of el-Lessiya, another of Tuthmosis III's understated foundations. A little further to the south, Ramses hailed the inscription which his father, the valiant Seti, had had engraved in the rock. He was determined, however, to go beyond rigor and rigidity, to humanize it and allow members of the royal family to participate in the immutable, impersonal image of Pharaoh. Before the sovereigns arrived, the governor and the notables had made their way to the quayside at Miam ahead of the royal procession, all bearing gifts of welcome.

Nubian craftsmen

The old capital was a vast storehouse for produce imported from the far south. It boasted many cabinet-makers, silversmiths, skin-dressers. Splendid chairs, seats, and stools were made from the hardwoods of Africa, encrusted with ivory and plated with gold. Cushions with cheetah-skin covers, ceremonial tail ornaments taken from giraffes and bulls, elaborate sandals with raised tips to protect the toes were all made there for the palace. Last but not least, there were the wonderfully carved toilet requisites—in particular, the strange assemblages of goldwork topped by statuettes of little Nubian boys climbing *dum*-palms. The sovereigns were presented with the finest of these products, together with the ritual offering of the celebrated dates from the land of gold.

Derr and Ibrim

On the right bank, before reaching Aniba, an agglomeration called Korosko marked the starting-point of an interminable caravan track that avoided the massive bend in the Nile and ended directly in the Sudan, near the site now called Abu Hamid. Ramses informed his viceroy of the time, Iuny, that he had chosen a place on this road east to erect a foundation devoted to Re-Horakhty—the current *hemispeos* of Derr. The sites for the future *hemispeos* dedicated to Ptah, Amun, and Re-Horakhty had already been chosen. There only remained the fourth divine entity of the set, Seth. This master of the Rameside ancestors was, as it were, embodied in the very person of Ramses at the holy site of Ibshek, the king and Nefertari's present destination, where the Horus of *Meha* was already venerated. Prior to this, the monarchs were to pass before the imposing rock of Ibrim to the south of Derr, at the foot of which three small niched chapels, each hewn from a single block, had been dug in honor of local manifestations of the divine and of the Tuthmosides.*

Thutmosid: Thutmosid Egypt lasted from the reign of Amenophis I until that of Thutmosis III.

Abu Simbel

Nefertari is spellbound

FOR NEFERTARI, THE LONG-AWAITED day was about to arrive. Since the crowning, she knew that her pharaoh, surpassing all that had been achieved before, nurtured the idea of creating two wholly subterranean sanctuaries in which, more than anywhere else, he could dedicate himself to participation in the essential rites. The protagonists would be Ramses and herself, in symbiosis with two elements necessary to the life of Egypt. To achieve this union, they would have to be drawn into the world of the gods, who would in turn impart their radiance to them and thereby sustain the life of the couple forever.

Still, the queen could never have imagined the spectacle that now greeted her. Digging in the local pink sandstone of the two mounds of Meha and Ibshek was already underway. The high-relief frontage of the larger *speos* of Meha to the south recalled that of the temples built in coursed stone. Framing the entrance, the queen would not have found the traditional two towers of the pylons, but instead four fantastic seated colossi, each sixty-five feet (twenty meters) high, the whole architectural scheme incorporated into a single trapezoid complex dominated by a row of twenty-two baboons standing in adoration of the sun. The workmen had already carved the bodies of these gigantic statues, each of which embodied aspects of the king's divinity and had its own special name.

Facing page:
High-relief frontage at the Meha, the most significant speos at Abu Simbel.

The mound of Ibshek to the north

To the north, the rock of Ibshek offered a quite different picture. The front consisted of six niches disposed in two groups flanking the opening to the *speos*. From afar, the queen would have spied six statues about twenty-six feet (eight meters) high, hewn out of the rock and occupying each niche. As the foundation was of less outlandish proportions than those of the southern *speos*, work here had

Pages 118–119:
Small temple devoted to the goddess Hathor and to Nefertari, wife of Ramses II. External view of the front, with its six statues of Ramses II and Nefertari. Abu Simbel.

made more progress. As Nefertari advanced, she would have recognized two statues of the king standing to either side of the entrance, each framed by two of her own sons—the eldest, Imenherkhepeshef, and Meryatum—likewise both standing but smaller in size.

At the southernmost point of the frontage, a statue of the king, slightly taller than the others, showed him standing and surrounded by the princes Meryatum and Meryre. At the northerrnmost point, the two royal children flanked a statue of the king sporting the headdress of the god Ta-tenen. And finally, between the two groups picturing Pharaoh on the north and south sections of the frontage, Nefertari would have seen her own radiant form topped by the headdress of Sothis, as if she was rising up irresistibly out of the mountain. She was accompanied, to right and left, by the two princesses, Merytamun and Henuttawy. She would have been struck by certain telling details: her own images were exactly same size as those of the king, and, in addition, the statuettes of her daughters were taller than those of her sons. In underscoring this tribute to the eminent role played by women so pointedly, Ramses showed considerable audacity.

The mound of Meha to the south

Conducted to the terrace of the great *speos*, the sovereigns were presented with yet another different spectacle: the four colossi were carved in a seated position, surrounded by two great royal ladies, two princes, and six as yet unmarried princesses (which suggests that the group was composed in the first quarter of the reign).

The façade

Nefertari and the queen dowager, *Mut*-Tuya, had pride of place twice each; then came the two elder sons of the two Great Royal Wives. Queen Isisnofret in person, however, was not represented. The reason is not hard to find: Nefertari had given birth to the eldest son, the crown prince, Imenherwenemef, who had become Imenherkhepeshef.

On the facade, the position of each member of the royal family exemplifies their importance in the eyes of Ramses, who had wanted to immortalize the sanctuaries of Ibshek and Meha as a memorial to his life's work. Thus, framing the southern colossus located close to the entrance door, first came Nefertari then, on other side, a statue of the queen mother. In parallel, near the northern colossus, were Nefertari, then the little princess Baketmut, daughter of Isisnofret. Lastly, between the legs of the first southern colossus, standing and holding a *flabellum*, an image of the eldest son Imenherkhepeshef had been carved, while Prince Ramses, son of Isisnofret, was placed before the first northern colossus. Between the legs of the second southern colossus appeared a little Isisnofret II, bearing the name of her mother, and to either side of the colossus, two other daughters of Isisnofret: Bentanat, the eldest, and Nebettawy. There remained the second northern colossus, between whose legs was represented the little Nefertari II, also bearing the name of her mother. To the left was Merytamun, eldest daughter of Nefertari and, on the far right, another statue of the queen mother, *Mut*-Tuya. The balance between all these personages was carefully calculated, with primacy being given to the mother of the crown prince and the queen dowager. To the south, priority was given to Nefertari's eldest son and Isisnofret's eldest daughter; to the north, to the eldest son of Isisnofret, Prince Ramses, and the eldest daughter of Nefertari. Precedence, then, had been respected, though—and this begs the question—there were two great absentees: the father, venerated but deceased, and the other Great Royal Wife of the time, who was to reappear later.

The great court

Once one passed through the narrow entrance door, the first underground room immediately recalled an open-air court, with the Osirid pillars of the traditional temple—except that here Ramses, in the Osirid attitude, wore the royal apron of the living. The scenes of war on the walls, affirming the determination of the master of Egypt to drive out evil from his borders, were almost complete. Draughtsmen had begun squaring up the huge scene recording the battle of Kadesh, which stretched over the entire northern wall of the hall. Facing this, the southern wall of the great court was to feature other images of "preventive" campaigns and referred to the king's past exploits. First came the seizure of a Syrian citadel, in which Pharaoh appears on his chariot, accompanied by three of his sons: Imenherkhepeshef, Ramses, and Pareherwenemef, each on their own smaller vehicle. Then followed the extermination of a Libyan chief and the image of the victorious sovereign installed in supreme majesty on his chariot and accompanied by his pet lion; in front of him, the two ranks of prisoners from the land of Kush is probably a reference to the repression in Irem during the time of the coregency. To conclude the military scenes illustrated to the south, Ramses offered his Kushite conquests as a tribute to the divine couple, Amun-Mut. The decorative register above the procession of the Kushite prisoners ended with an image as significant as it is original. There, one could admire Amun of Napata in his rocky sanctuary. Beneath his seated effigy passed the body of an immense cobra, drawing

Ramses II on his chariot accompanied by his lion. Bas-relief at the Temple of Ramses II, Abu Simbel.

itself up between Amun and Ramses honoring the divinity—without doubt an image of the Nile meandering from its sources and preparing to dispense its generous flood waters over the land of Pharaoh. Addressing this, and following the battle of Kadesh, Ramses presents himself before Horakhty and Iusas—one of the forms of Hathor—trailing two rows of Hittite prisoners behind him. Once more Pharaoh makes a point of stressing the importance of his offspring, already numerous at that stage (the sixth and seventh years) of his reign. Carvings of processions of the first sons and daughters appear on the lower reaches of the walls framing the entrance door.

The hypostyle

The main purpose of the hypostyle hall after the great court was to depict on its south and north walls the barque of Amun, adorned with the sacred ram's head, together with that of Re, decorated with the falcon head, so that the royal couple could pay them homage. In truth, this was the ship of Amun-Re, but divided in two; moreover, to receive this unique cultic vessel a plinth had been arranged in the floor of the Holy of Holies. An image of Amun-Re's barque was planned for the southern wall of this latter room, while that of the deified Ramses appeared on the north. In this last image one could also see Horakhty. Similarly, in the small rock vault to the south of the Great Temple, the barque of Amun was replaced on the southern wall by that of Thoth, evoking the Flood which he controlled and revived, like Amun himself in whom the king was incarnate.

Lighting the Holy of Holies

The axis had been so devised that, twice a year, the earliest rays of the rising sun would first strike one of the seated statues planned

Great Temple of Abu Simbel, from the great court to the sanctuary where Ramses is enthroned with the tri-unity.

Sanctuary with statues of Ramses and the gods Ptah, Amun, and Re-Horakhty. Great Temple, Abu Simbel.

for the wall at the rear of the sanctuary. There were also plans for carving in the solid rock—from south to north—likenesses of Ptah, Amun, Ramses, and, finally, Re-Horakhty. As the sun moved, rising each day a little more to the north at the approach of the summer solstice and a little more to the south with the coming of that of winter, the sun's rays would only penetrate into the heart of the temple during two periods of the year. From January 10 to March 30, the sun "sweeps round," and, on February 20, its rays pass along the axis of the temple, falling progressively on three of the statues. Then, between September 10 and November 30, direct penetration along the axis of the Holy of Holies occurs—on October 20. On February 20, therefore, the illumination starts with the statue of Amun, with the light passing on to the effigy of the king. Contrariwise, on October 20 the sun initially illuminates the statue of Re-Horakhty, before moving again to the statue of Ramses. Twice a year, then, the two divine forms transmit to the sovereign the radiant light necessary to sustain his divinely imbued nature, which might otherwise lessen in intensity during the year. In this manner, the king is illumined by Amun and Re; their barque is his barque, and it is this boat which must then descend the Nile on New Year's Day, since it is the image, the symbol, of the "genius" of the Flood itself.

As for the statue of Ptah—the god who emerges from darkness and who conjures it up—the sun merely brushes his left shoulder.

The role of the small speos

In the blessed rocky outcrop chosen by Ramses, however, miracles were not confined to these magical periods of the year. The sanctuary of Hathor, dedicated to the queen, was to complement another major event. Dedicated to femininity, the cave with Hathor capitals, in which the reliefs literally overflow with charm and youth as nowhere else, recalls the sovereigns at the beginning of their reign, and their youthful appearance adds still more to the sanctuary's poetry. The sanctum was thus precisely defined, as expressed by the culminating image of the sacred cow of Hathor at the rear of the Holy of Holies—a direct allusion to the annual revivification of the king associated with the returning Flood, which the goddess seems to draw out from the very mountainside. To make this possible, the rites had to pass through an initial stage in the person of the female sovereign at these specially chosen sites. She appeared, upright and slender, on one of the walls, receiving from Hathor (Eros) and from Isis (maternity) the crown of Sothis, the star that vanishes and reappears, thereby triggering the return of the sun at the beginning of each year.

This is why the name of the *speos*, engraved in columns of hieroglyphics on the front, was composed by Pharaoh in the following terms: "Nefertari, by the love of whom the sun rises." Finally, the proper functioning of this cosmic progression was to be guaranteed by the solar altar planned for the north of the great *speos*.

Head of Hathor on a pillar, Temple of Nefertari, Abu Simbel.

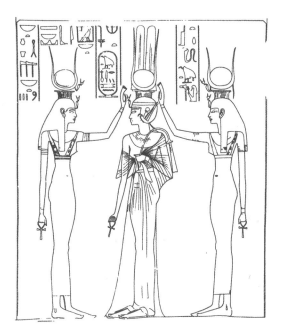

Transformation of Nefertari into Sothis (Sirius) under the care of Hathor and Isis in Mount Ibshek, Small Temple of Nefertari, Abu Simbel.

5

THE PATH
TO PEACE

Moab and Edom

O N HIS RETURN FROM UPPER EGYPT, Ramses quickly realized the extent to which news of events at the battle of Kadesh had spread throughout Canaan and how it must have preyed on the minds of the onetime vassals of the "Two Crowns," as well as giving the incorrigible Shasu Bedoins something to think about. His real concern was now focused on eastern Palestine, to the east and south of the Dead Sea, where the populations of Moab and Edom (Seir) had become aware of their identity and rejected Egyptian dominion. It was necessary at all costs to quash resistance in these regions—they were all too close to the borders and, won over by a skillful Hittite propaganda war, could at any time foment disorder—in order thereafter to move on to retake Amurru, a key buffer state in securing the country against a new coalition.

War in the land of Moab: circling movement as executed by Ramses II and his son Imenherkhepeshef, which came together at Rabath Batora.

The prime objective was to eliminate resistance in the territories encircling the Dead Sea over a broad front. Prince Imenherkhepeshef, enjoined by his father, who had seen his worth in the field, to march his troops eastwards to south of the Dead Sea, was to seize on the road back Rabath Batora (formerly Butartu) in Edom (Seir). In the other direction, meanwhile, Ramses was crossing the center of Canaan to the west of the Dead Sea and had pushed on to its northern limits, leaving Urusalim (future Jerusalem) to his right, before descending once again to the east of the Dead Sea in modern-day Jordan to take the town of Dibon. Progressing southwards, he joined forces with his eldest son, who seems to have awaited him at Rabath Batora, all the while endeavoring to pacify the region.

The way was free, then, to push on more or less directly towards the north, without meeting any particular resistance, in the direction of the province of Upi that Ramses had lost after the battle of Kadesh. He stopped at Temesq (another Pi-Ramesse, today Damascus), before moving on, it would seem, to the city of Kumidi. This route was called "the road of the king."

Did the Exodus occur under Ramses II? (1272–1271 BCE)

T HESE SORTIES, THE STARTING POINT for which was the north of Sinai, had sparked agitation in the region. From generation to generation, the Shasu Bedouins, and more especially the semi-nomadic Apiru (or Habiru), "the dusty ones," who have been linked to the Heperer ("Hebrews"), had passed down various tales that soon fused and grew into legend.

Could, then, the origin of the Exodus be situated in this period? Nothing precise in the Egyptian texts permits us to pinpoint it. Nevertheless, the biblical name of the city Ramses can naturally be linked to that of Pi-Ramesse, for the construction of which Apiru are known to have been employed, along with the soldiers of the king, "to drag stones to the Pylon of the Palace of Ramses II," and to many other monuments.

Was Moses an Egyptian?

The name Moses, coming from Mose (*mes*, "child," *mesy*, "to bring into the world," etc.), also forms the derivation of other theophoric* names, such as Thotmes, Rames, etc. Many Egyptians, to the Nineteenth Dynasty, bore the name of Mes (or Mose). Admittedly, at that period, as in the Eighteenth Dynasty, Asian prisoners were sometimes employed in the great royal programs of excavation and construction. Furthermore, prisoners of war were not only ones who could be turned into an effective labor force: large numbers of perfectly free Asians and Bedouins would offer their services as workmen and laborers, like the Apiru who made bricks or hauled construction stone for the Pi-Ramesse, or else as seasonal workers for the grape-harvest.

Theophoric: relating to the gods.

Foreign manpower under Pharaoh

LIKE CERTAIN MANUMITTED prisoners, some of these workers settled permanently in Egypt; crucially, their children would be educated in the local manner, so that following study in the *kep* of the palace or of the royal harem, sons of foreign chiefs would return to their native land imbued with Egyptian culture. Many carved out a career in the country and could be found in the immediate entourage of Pharaoh. It is not inconceivable, therefore, that Moses was one of these, and the Acts of the Apostles (7:22) note that Moses was educated "in all the wisdom of the Egyptians and was mighty in words and deeds," having been raised in the court to adulthood (Exodus 2: 10–11). It should not be forgotten that, from time immemorial, Egyptians were known to be nationalistic but were exempt from xenophobia. In the written documentation of the Nineteenth Dynasty, examples exist which show, for example, that an Egyptian lady freed three of her "slaves" before adopting them. Thus, Moses presented as the adopted son of a daughter of Pharaoh is not beyond the bounds of possibility.

An indispensable workforce?

T HIS BRINGS US TO THE QUESTION of on what serious criteria one might base the notion of an "exodus" of immigrant workers— especially an exodus that Pharaoh is said to have opposed, even going so far as to pursue the escapees at a time when his immediate major concerns were of a more elevated nature than losing a section of the labor force, which could always be replaced. There is, in fact, no event in Egyptian documents recording the expulsion—or departure—of foreigners from the country at that time. In the final analysis, a hypothesis may be ventured, if one places the beginning of the Exodus during the period immediately prior to the expedition of Ramses and his son as they prepared to cross the Negev towards Edom: Pharaoh could well have refused to release the Apiru, who might then have joined forces with the Shasu, something which could have hampered the free movement of the Egyptian troops.

The plagues of Egypt?

A MONG THE "PLAGUES" VISITED upon Egypt, it seems, in order to convince Pharaoh to permit the departure of the Hebrews, the Bible records a layer of ash that spread over the land. Perhaps this is an echo of the aftermath of some distant cataclysm, such as an eruption on the island of Santorini, volcanic debris from which could have floated to the north of the Sinai. There are also details in the biblical text that fit in neither with the customs nor with the environment of the land of Pharaoh. For instance, the idea of putting to death all first-born male children might be Asian, or even Phoenician, but it is certainly not Egyptian. As for the plagues of locusts, though massively harmful in North Africa, in Egypt the insect is generally considered beneficial, a weapon against evil that appears in prophylactic tomb decorations as early as the Old Kingdom.

The views of Egyptologists

E VEN THIS BRIEF ANALYSIS BRINGS out one point: the account would seem to be the result of a mishmash of independent facts taken from various eras collected very late on; it probably concerns what—to Egyptian eyes, at least—was a relatively minor event, which was then recast to form a coherent, "heroic" account. The historian K. A. Kitchen claims that the biblical Exodus is not even hinted at in

Ramses' proud inscriptions, and he is inclined to situate a possible reminiscence of what has been called the Exodus in the reign of Ramses II—an inconsequential if unsavory incident, later transformed by the Hebrews into a more memorable episode.

For his part, M. Bietak, who has been investigating the *hyksos* site of Avaris for years, sees the Proto-Israelites as part of the Shasu quoted in the Egyptian texts, but thinks that the Exodus occurred before the fifth year of the reign of Merenptah. D. Redford, meanwhile, is of the opinion that the Exodus legend does not reflect the Egyptian situation during the Eighteenth and Nineteenth Dynasties, but instead that of the Twenty-Sixth—the writer, in his view, being familiar with the topography of the delta during the dynasty in question and at the beginning of the Persian era. His conclusion is that only the broad outline of the narrative, composed well after the events, can be accepted.

What is clear, then, is that the available evidence is thin on the ground and rather inconclusive.

The Exodus: an attempt at a reconstitution

ULTIMATELY, AND TAKING ACCOUNT of studies undertaken with the greatest prudence and objectivity, one might conclude that, if there was a skirmish, or perhaps a conflict, between Pharaoh's authorities and a group of workers of Semitic origin who downed tools and fled Egypt, the event took on major significance only for the Apiru (undoubtedly the future Hebrews), who placed it at the beginning of their history. What follows represents an attempt to reconstitute events which, willy-nilly, were to be indissolubly linked to Ramesside Egypt.

At the dawn of the Nineteenth Dynasty, Pharaoh had to handle relations with his near neighbors with care. As for Moses, he was certainly one of the young Semites raised in the palace in the Egyptian manner, so that thereafter "the man Moses was very great in the land of Egypt, in the sight of Pharaoh's servants, and in the sight of the people" (Exodus 11:3). One day, he witnessed a drubbing meted out by a foreman to one his compatriots (Exodus 2), at the period Seti I was working on Pi-Ramesse. Moses came between the workman and his foreman, whom he struck fatally. He then failed to hand himself in and fled in fear of judgment. One imagines him wandering through the country of Madian, where he marries the daughter of the region's high priest, witnesses the burning bush, and receives the supernatural order to lead the Hebrews out of Egypt

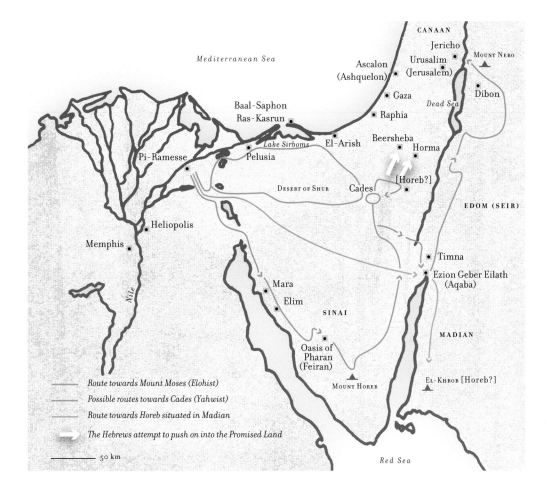

Map showing the various
possible routes taken
during the Exodus.

(Ex. 3:13–15). The death of Seti I occurred at just the right time for
Moses to try to return to Egypt and carry out the divine instructions
he had been given. The new Pharaoh, Ramses, one can't help sus-
pecting, had been unaware of, or had pardoned, the death of the foreman at Moses' hand.

Moses once again rose to an eminent place in the entourage of the
master of Egypt and soon plucked up courage to ask permission to
lead his people on a three-day march into the desert so as to make a
sacrifice. Though certainly no warrior, Moses, sure of his authority
and inspired by his god, does not appear to have taken into consideration any possible misgivings on the part of Pharaoh. The murder of
an Egyptian; the sudden loss of a labor force to which Egypt had
opened her doors; complete disregard for the position of the country
following the loss of Amurru, the hostilities at its borders and the

plots being hatched by the Hittites: there was a lot to raise Pharaoh's ire, and this is what duly occurred. Moses, however, benefiting from circumstances favorable to his aims, then violently contradicts Pharaoh, and, so we are told, issues threats and calls down scourges on Egypt before which the sovereign is ultimately obliged to bow. Then follows the exodus from Egypt, after the alleged death of Pharaoh's eldest son that constituted the tenth plague of Egypt. The Hebrews (Apiru?) are then "expelled." The Yahwist account has them leave directly from Pi-Ramesse (Ramses), after Moses enjoins them, among other things, to gather together all their wealth.

The troop then proceeded by the road of the Philistines, in direction of Cades (to the south of the Negev), before receiving orders to retrace its steps. The Hebrews returned in the direction of Baal-Saphon (Ras-Kasrun), a place with an extremely perilous reputation. Finally, the "expelled" group penetrates deep into the desert of Shur.

There is a second tradition, the Elohist, that follows the Exodus (E) source. It seems more logical, since it rejects the route along the fortified Mediterranean coast, far too dangerous for the Apirus as it was peppered with Egyptian citadels. In this version, the fleeing party would have traveled south, in direction of the oasis of Ayun Mussa ("Moses' spring"), then the oasis of Pharaoh (Feizan). Mount Horeb would be located still further to the south. Nonetheless, the setting of the ancient Jewish site of pilgrimage in the Sinai is not known with certainty. The Yahwists locate it on Mount Horeb, where Moses experienced revelation, not far from Cades, in Gebel Halal. The Elohists place it to the south, its inspired mass towering over the site where a monastery-fortress would later be founded by Justinian, dedicated in the ninth century to St. Catherine, martyred in 296 CE.

Whether driven out or fleeing, the group, according to both traditions, would have gathered near Cades, before entering Canaan. The refugees, however, were not at the end of their arduous adventure, since they now met hostility on the part of the king of Edom (Seir), who refused to let them through. They were thus forced to head north and circumvent Edom and Moab, and then overcome the Amorites. From Mount Nebo where the Hebrews finally arrived after forty years of wandering, "miracles," and ordeals, Moses was able to set eyes, before his death, on Urusalim and the Promised Land.

In the current state of knowledge, it seems rash to propose a precise date for the Exodus. Still, the few clues we have make it possible to situate the event at the beginning of the reign of Ramses II. Logically, it would have been during the period in the seventh year of his reign when Ramses and Imenherkhepeshef went on their dual "punitive" expedition to Edom and Moab. Clues, though, are few and far between. One remark, however: that campaign coincided with the quarrel between the Hebrews and Edom, and with certain points on their journey through these regions to which the Bible alludes.

The Libyan neighbors

S HORTLY AFTER KADESH, AS SOON as Ramses had decided to re-organize his army, training camps were set up in the western zone of the delta, where incursions were feared. The aim was to forestall attacks by equipping the area with a chain of strongholds, over several hundred kilometers, similar to those built for the defense of Nubia or for the "Wall of the Prince" on the eastern fringes of the delta. The movements and operations of the Egyptian troops, led by officers trained in modern tactics, provided information about the terrain and about the life and customs of those crossing it in the direction of Egypt. Investigations carried out in these regions by the Egyptian Egyptologist Labib Habachi have revealed the existence of three forts, incorporating as usual buildings for the troops, a commander's residence, and a temple.

Ramses, quarrymen, and artists

I N ADDITION TO INSPECTING the borders of Libya, painstakingly preparing the expedition to retake the cities of Galilee, and devising punishments for the rebels of Amurru on account of their continuous treason, Ramses also made a point of prospecting for quarries in person. Moreover, he had decided to apply himself to instituting and propagating the innovations of his father in the social field. One comes across evidence in the texts of his concern for the wellbeing of his craftsmen, and of the care he took to establish an equitable wage scale. The country was gradually being introduced to humane policies.

In the eighth year of his reign, then, Ramses began prospecting for quarries. He traveled out into the desert, very near the "Red Mountain," Gebel Ahmar: "it was at this point in time that His Majesty found an enormous block, such as had never been discovered since the reign of Re: it was taller than a granite obelisk!" This could certainly form the raw material for a new colossus whose name he also supplied, "Ramses-beloved-of-Amun, the god," and whose realization, he says, he entrusted to "élite workmen, skilled with their hands." Completed by the ninth year of his reign, this beneficent colossus extended its divine royal protection over the whole land, while Pharaoh himself set about fortifying its borders. Ramses continued his explorations in the surroundings among the veins of quarzite, discovering "those which resemble mer wood, red in color, for carving statues for the Temple of Ptah [Memphis]. . . . Other statues [were made] for the Temple of Amun 'Ramses-beloved-of-Amun' and for that Temple of Ptah of 'Ramses-beloved-of-Amun' with Pi-Ramesse 'Great-with-Victories.' "

Leaving the delta, the king did not forget the south of the country, a region he cherished, and traveled in the island of Elephantine. There he located various quarries, naming them as soon as they were discovered. Hence there was the quarry of "Ramses-beloved-of-Amun-beloved-like-Ptah," the quarry of "Usermaatre-Setepenre-sovereign-of-the-Two-Lands", and the quarry of "Ramessu-beloved-of-Amun-beloved-like-Re." Betraying Ramses' concern to play to the full his role as father of his country, over whose wellbeing he watches vigilantly, the narrative is supplemented by an account of his satisfaction with a piece of work that started in the most favorable conditions, as well as the announcement of richly deserved and fair remuneration for the workforce. As Ramses declares: "I commit myself to meeting all your needs. . . . thus, for you the granaries overflow with wheat, so that you will not spend a single day without food. . . ."

A schedule of works for the anticipated absence of the sovereign was then drawn up: since the generous pay policy would ensure the welfare of many workmen, the activity was going to be beneficial to all.

Syria regained

T HE RECENT EXPEDITION TO THE south of Palestine had borne fruit. In Galilee and Canaan it had demonstrated that Ramses was returning to the fray with undimmed determination; for this reason, resistance on Pharaoh's arrival was limited. By the end of the eighth and during the ninth year of his reign, around 1271 BCE, Ramses was advancing unimpeded along the coast. The Hittites, it seems, did nothing to oppose the return of the Egyptians to these outposts in the south of Phoenicia.

In the north of Gaza, Ramses seized back Ascalon (Ashquelon), as well as some other Canaanite cities. Then, proceeding towards the north of Amurru, Ramses skirted round Kadesh, the city that he had never been able to retake, and which remained a thorn in his flesh.

Facing page:
Colossus of Ramses II.
Temple of Ptah, Memphis.

The first seizure of Dapur

A MONG PHARAOH'S RELATIVELY SHORT-LIVED victories at the end of the eighth year of his reign, his finest conquest, compared to the smattering of minor citadels taken along the route depicted on the western face of the First Pylon of Ramesseum, was the town of Dapur to the south of Aleppo, in the territory of the city-state of Tunip. Of all the fortified towns which, susceptible to Hittite propaganda, had risen up, Dapur assumed the greatest importance in Ramses' eyes, for it constituted the northernmost stronghold in the zone of Hittite penetration he had been able to acquire.

On two occasions, he had a glorious picture of the seizure of the city made: on the west wall of the first court at the temple at Luxor; and more especially, in a remarkable departure, on the southeastern wall of the hypostyle hall in his jubilee temple, the Ramesseum. The left part of the composition shows the king on a heroic scale, leading his two horses and loosing arrows into a pile of enemy dead

The first capture of Dapur. Ramesseum, Thebes-West.

Pharaoh's chariot crushing the enemy. Ramesseum, Thebes-West.

brought down from their chariots as they try to escape back into the citadel. Dressed in long, narrow robes, Ramses' adversaries are all Hittite in type, with receding chins and a heavy pony-tail falling down their backs. The right part of the image presents a citadel of a type very different from that of an Egyptian or even Amorite forti- fied town being stormed by Egyptian soldiers and Sherden. On the lower reaches, four kinds of conical screens in the form of cara- paces borne on stakes can be made out. They had been erected so as to protect Ramses's young sons (Meryamun, Imenemwia, Seti, and Setepenre), who appear to be straining to join in the skirmish. Two other princes, whose names are not indicated, climb, shield in hand, up a tall ladder to reach the second floor of the fortification. The top levels are occupied by last-ditch defenders firing arrows and throwing stones.

Then comes the last episode—the capitulation. Two of Ramses' elder sons, Khaemwaset and Montuherkhepeshef, prepare to cut the throats of the enemy chiefs. This time, the banner flying from

Below top: *the besieged forces throw stones from the fortifications.*

Below center: *Egyptians attack the fortress with ladders.*

Below bottom: *battle scene.*

the summit of the fortified city is shown peppered with arrows, thus confirming the seizure of the city.

Carved by the finest artists, who have combined singular freedom of expression with consummate elegance, the bas-reliefs, exploring every detail of the action, reveal a masterly sense of composition.

The warriors' reward

During the battles in Galilee and in Amurru in the eighth year of his reign, Egyptian soldiers and foreign mercenaries alike—including the Sherden—had proved equal to every situation. It was a disciplined, motivated, and victorious band, and now, just as back home Ramses had paid well for the qualities of his craftsmen, he had to remunerate or reward his officers and men. He later went on to present them with land, but on his return in the ninth year of his reign he was, above all, to offer them public honors. Numerous steles were engraved for the occasion, with admirable scenes of the king distributing cups, necklaces, and other gold objects to his valorous soldiers while the populace celebrated.

The counter-offensive of the confederation

During Ramses's latest campaign to northern Syria, it appears that the Hittite Muwatallis, probably at death's door, had neither the intention nor the ability to put together a new coalition. It is, however, beyond all doubt that he did send reinforcements to his allies, chiefly to the princes of Aleppo and Karkemish; but these had

Ramses, mounted on one of his colossi, throws various valuables down to the assembled soldiers. Lower section of a stele of Qantir. Roemer- und Pelizaeus- Museum, Hildesheim.

not been enough to protect the fortress. Still, upon Pharaoh's departure and his return to Egypt, the small Egyptian garrison left in position was insufficient to withstand attacks from the Khatti's neighbors, and the fortifications were again taken; and, since they had been unable to capture the man himself, Ramses' effigy was seized.

Dapur again retaken

R AMSES NOW FOUND HIMSELF FORCED, yet again, to set out with his troops to reaffirm the supremacy of Egyptian power at this strategic point in the Middle East. Towards 1270–1269 BCE, he again passed close to Nahr el-Kelb, where he had a third stele erected. With fire in his loins, he led an attack so lightning-fast that, as soon as he arrived on the battleground, he leapt off his chariot and, on foot, took up a position at the head of his men, loosing his death-dealing arrows right outside the citadel (as the relief in the temple at Luxor shows).

He emerged, it seems, unscathed and once again sallied into Dapur. After the departure of Pharaoh, however, the Syrian cities once more fell under the sway of their powerful neighbor.

The death of Muwatallis

I T CAN IN ALL LIKELIHOOD BE SUPPOSED that, by this time, Ramses regretted not having lent a more receptive ear to the peace offerings made by Muwatallis in the aftermath of Kadesh. The moment was no longer propitious, since the "Sun of Khatti" had just expired

Second battle of Dapur. Luxor.

and his successor, the son of one of his concubines, had mounted the throne—illegitimately, it would seem. This prince, Urhi-Teshub, enthroned under the name Mursilis (Mursil) III, was a colorless character who took against his uncle Hattusilis, a stronger personality whom he had packed off to the north of the kingdom. Mursilis III began his reign in an atmosphere of intrigue and scheming, limiting his personal action strictly to within the borders of his land. More than before, Ramses was now of the opinion that diplomacy would ensure a greater measure of security than courageous expeditions that cost a great deal in manpower, to the detriment of his people's welfare and prosperity. It was far wiser to consolidate his firmly acquired positions, make the most of dissension among the Hittites, and thereby set up a status quo beyond the zone he had the means of controlling durably. For the following six years, then, action on behalf of Egyptian governors gradually replaced armed repression, and order was maintained in Canaan and in part of Amurru.

Statue of Wennofer, high priest of Osiris. Musée du Louvre, Paris.

The wellbeing of the country

I N THE TENTH YEAR OF HIS REIGN, Ramses, back from a fresh campaign in Syria, no longer entertained any hopes of retaking Amurru by arms: he had resolutely turned to more diplomatic solutions, in order to forestall events which might, sooner or later, threaten his borders. Revenue regularly came in from tax collection—as much in the homelands as in offices belonging to the governors of Asia or the viceroy of Nubia. The Two Lands were all opulence and calm.

During the twelfth year of his reign, the pontificate of Nebwennef, high priest of Amun in Karnak, had run its course, so Ramses proceeded to appoint a new incumbent in the person of Wennofer, father of the faithful Imeneminet. On returning to Thebes after the ceremony, he was careful to visit the construction sites for the temples with which he was gradually enriching his lands. That of Akhmim was particularly dear to his heart. The city had been home to the family of Tiyi, principal wife of Amenophis (Amenhotep) III, of whose indisputable influence on her son, Amenophis IV (Akhenaten), Ramses was well aware. Around the city's main temple, its priest-scholars, with close links to the clergy at Hermopolis, had long formed a hotbed of astronomical studies, where the brother of Tiyi, Aanen, had been educated. Ramses II had also made a point of consulting these tireless scholars when founding his temples, especially those of

Abu Simbel and the Ramesseum. He had taken the decision to set up another sanctuary in the city: once the pylons had been built, he would visit the new quarries himself and have them embellished with colossi showing him surrounded by his elder daughters, foremost among whom was Merytamun.

Revolt in Irem

EVEN BEFORE HE WAS BACK IN Pi-Ramesse, a messenger from the viceroy of Nubia, Iuny, caught up with him to inform him of disorder on the horizon in distant Irem, in the region of the Third Cataract. As usual, Ramses' reaction was immediate. He dispatched forces drawn from the division of Amun and barracked in Thebes, delegating to head the troops, in addition to the viceroy, four of his sons undergoing military training at Memphis, including Sethemwia and Khaemwaset. To serve as an example to the land of Kush, the king ordered a summary of the punitive expedition to be depicted on the walls of the great door to the viceroy's new residence in Amara-West: the capture of seven thousand rebels in a very short space of time. Pharaoh's congratulations to his viceroy were moderate, and the official was instructed to inspect the province to the far south more regularly. No further incidents occurred.

The choice of royal sons for the war

THE FACT THAT RAMSES' ELDEST SON, Imenherkhepeshef, had taken part neither in the sieges and battles at Dapur, nor in the repression of Irem, has been taken to mean that the crown prince had disappeared from the scene after the great Palestine expedition in the seventh and eighth years of his reign (1272–1271 BCE). Such an absence could, on the contrary, lend credence to an intention on Ramses' part to advance the sons of Isisnofret during the seizure of Dapur, since the sons of Nefertari, Imenherkhepeshef, and Pareherwenemef, had already had an opportunity to prove their mettle precociously at Kadesh. The latter prince was declared First Champion of the army and bore the title of First Charioteer to the King, as did the fifth royal son, Montuherkhepeshef. As for the repression of the incidents in Irem, which had not been serious enough to demand the royal presence, there the job had been shared out equitably between Sethemwia, his eighth son, born to Nefertari, and Merenptah, his thirteenth son, born to Isisnofret.

Prince Khaemwaset sporting the wig and necklace of a high priest of Ptah. Serapeum, Memphis.

Khaemwaset, Great Priest of Ptah at Memphis, presents to the Bull, Apis, whose funerals he directs, materials for the "opening of the mouth and the eyes." Serapeum, Saqqara. Musée du Louvre, Paris.

The royal son with undoubtedly the most literary bent, Khaemwaset, son of Isisnofret, had played a key role at the time of the surrender of the city of Dapur, but had soon entered the service of Ptah of Memphis. Aged twenty, having become *sem* priest and having caught the eye of the high priest, in the nineteenth year of Ramses' reign, in company of Vizier Paser and General Ramses, his brother, he had been present at the sumptuous entombment of the first Apis bull to die during his father's reign.

The diplomacy of Ramses and conflict in the Middle East

Ramses' intelligence services observed the initially simmering, then openly hostile, struggle between Mursilis III and his uncle Hattusilis with the greatest interest. The final rupture between the two men occurred when the nephew settled in the capital Hattusha and attempted to deprive Hattusilis of the last few minor states over which his rule still held sway.

Aided by his partisans, Hattusilis now opposed Mursilis III's depredations and captured him. Showing leniency, instead of condemning his rival to death he merely sent him into exile to Nukhashshe, south of Aleppo in northern Syria. Meanwhile, Ramses had formed an alliance with the king of Babylon, Kadashman-Turgu, before making approaches to Salmanasar I, the Assyrian overlord.

In the eighteenth year of his reign, benefiting from a positive turn in proceedings, he agreed to offer refuge to Mursilis III, who had "escaped" from his exile and had apparently applied for asylum to Pharaoh. The suspicion arises that Ramses had manipulated events to bring such a situation about. Hattusilis might fear fresh conflict with his nephew, seconded this time by a very powerful enemy. He was assured nevertheless of the loyalty of the king of Babylon, Kadashman-Turgu, who opted to sever diplomatic relations with Egypt. Ramses now held an important asset, which he decided to use against the Hittite. He felt the hour had come to exact a long-awaited revenge, and began mobilizing the troops on which he counted to train his vassals in Beth Shan and Mageddo, in Canaan.

Undaunted at Beth Shan, he awaited the harbingers of an attack from the new Hittite coalition, which never came. He then vowed to commemorate this new adventure beyond the borders of Egypt with the erection of another stele at Beth Shan.

The Hittites' enforced retreat

ALWAYS ON HIS GUARD, RAMSES WAS still awaiting a reaction from the Hittite. The eighteenth year of his reign had begun, and the information coming to him through his zealous advisors caused him to take heart. Asia Minor generally was experiencing considerable upheaval. The role of renegade was initially embraced by Shattuara II, prince of Mitanni (Hanigalbat). Having sworn loyalty to Assyria, he had betrayed King Salmanasar I and joined with the Hittites, in cahoots with his ally, the king of Karkemish. The Assyrians consequently went on the attack, completely destroying the glorious Karkemish, as well as nine other citadels of importance, and plundering a hundred and eighty colonies. Without landing a blow, Ramses could now reap the rewards of an excellent economic outlook and guarantee the security of his country. North of the Euphrates, the borders of Assyria ran into those of the Hittite, who had also seized the Syrian provinces. Ramses realized that Hattusilis, caught on the back foot, could no longer pose a threat. He now had another diplomatic task in front of him—all the more so since there were hints that his adversary was prepared to make contact with the adroit informal envoys who were sounding the Hittite king out to see if his intentions were peaceful.

New Great Royal Wives

R AMSES POSSESSED A RATHER impressive number of secondary wives, Egyptian but more especially Asiatic, the results of agreements concluded with his vassals, together with daughters of chiefs of the land of Wawat: the concubines who filled the "Houses of Women" were by now beyond counting. Naturally, the harem of Mi-Ur, near the picturesque lake of Fayum and overseen by the queen mother, was the site of sumptuous residences for the Great Royal Wives, the little princes and the first royal daughters, offspring of the principal spouses; but other harems were also established in the provinces ready to receive visits from Pharaoh. His two Great Royal Wives, Nefertari and Isisnofret, had already borne him many princes and princesses. The first children, whom he had made a point of

Right:
Merytamun, daughter of Ramses II. Façade of the Great Temple, Abu Simbel, Thebes-West.

Far right:
Bentanat, daughter of Ramses II; bas-relief from Memphis. Egyptian Museum, Cairo.

depicting on the frontages of both *speos* in Meha and Ibshek, and inside the great court of Meha, had now turned into adults. The two elder girls were in their turn soon to receive the title of Great Royal Wife, without this in the least "unseating" their venerated mothers. The elder daughter of Isisnofret, Bentanat, was the first to be promoted in this way. This same year saw the completion of the sacred caves of Meha and Ibshek in the land of Wawat. In honor of the event, Ramses had an image of this princess carved with her name accompanied by a new title: *hemet-nesut-weret*, "Great Royal Wife."

The elevation of Nefertari's eldest daughter, Merytamun, soon followed. Here, however, a problem arose. All the walls and pillars of the great court of the larger *speos*, reserved for what one might call the "family album," had already been filled. Thus, the viceroy of Nubia, Hekanakht, had to represent the scene commemorating the princess's recent promotion on one of the walls of the mount of Meha. There one can still see Nefertari receiving the viceroy's homage, while the king, accompanied by young Merytamun, makes an offering to the divine triad.

The inauguration of Meha and Ibshek

T HE FAMILY GROUP AROUND RAMSES now comprised first and foremost the queen dowager, the four Great Royal Wives, then the princes and princesses, offspring of the first two Great Wives. In this, the nineteenth year of Ramses' reign, all were to attend the festivities inaugurating both *speos* of Abu Simbel—in other words, the act of "Giving the House to its Master,"* a ceremony which in point of fact here fulfilled a special role, due to the nature of the sanctuaries and their exceptional function.

The message of the temples

E ACH YEAR, WHEN THE STAR SOTHIS (Sirius) once again shone on the horizon after seventy days of invisibility, it would bring the sun up with it. This period marked the rebirth of the daystar and the return of Osiris, appearing as the life-bringing waters of *Hapy*, the Flood. The continuance of this cyclical phenomenon had to be guaranteed by the actions of Pharaoh, whose essential role was to ensure its smooth progress by performing suitable rituals. In creating the two sacred caves to the north of the Second Cataract, close to the zone where the Nile enters Egyptian Nubia, Ramses' intention had been to create a mythical site where the New Year's Day miracle could be played out. The beginning of the year (July 18–20) conjured up the reappearance of Sothis and the providential onset of the Flood. Independently of their historical signification, and so as to give concrete form to the king's cosmic plans, the two sanctuaries acted jointly to illustrate a phenomenon without which Egypt would simply not exist. The purpose of their presence at this site was above all to evoke the sun's reemergence into the world, revived at the dawn of the New Year by the divine body that had already been called, five thousand years previously, the Dog Star.

The sun was incarnated in Ramses (Usermaatre), who dominates the door of the great temple in the form of a falcon-headed man adorned with the solar disc (Re) and supported by the symbols *user* and *maat*. As for the star Sothis, Ramses wanted his kingdom to identify it with Nefertari, she who had given birth to the heir to the throne, Imenherkhepeshef. To play this role, she had been invested by two of the female manifestations of the divine: Hathor and Isis. Everything in the cave of Ibshek, where this divine avatar is represented—the figures, offerings, flowers, the royal couple praying to the goddess Ta-Uret (Taweret, "the Great") and asking for a happy birth (of the year)—is suffused with femininity.

Ramses and Nefertari make offerings to "the Great One" (Tueris) for a prosperous New Year. Ibshek, Abu Simbel.

*Ramses-Re-Harakhty
dominates the frontage
of Meha. Abu Simbel,
Thebes-West.*

The spectacle

FOLLOWING THE MYSTERIOUS CEREMONIES in the Holy of Holies,
at dawn on the prescribed day the final rite was a mime performed
by the royal couple before the two caves and in the presence of the
priests of the Nile and the worthies of the court, accompanied by the
royal family. Only then would the Inundation occur. On the front of
Ibshek, the luminous statue of Nefertari, sporting the majestic Sothis
headdress, seems to emerge like the star on the horizon, while, towering over the entrance to the major sanctuary, Ramses-Re-Horakhty
can be seen as a metaphor for the light of the world in the firmament.

*Pages 150–151:
Temples of Ramses II
and Nefertari. Abu Simbel,
Thebes-West.*

Now the divine barque of Thoth—the barque of Time, kept in a room dug out of the very rock outside and south of the temple—was to be loaded onto the royal barge, which would bring back it to Egypt, a symbol of the Flood provoked by Pharaoh. The reception of the barque was celebrated in Thebes, to coincide with the arrival of the Flood. In the Ramesseum, the divine vessels would be drawn from the temple on poles borne by priests and taken out to honor the hidden power which now made its reappearance. Ramses could then be shown as the guarantor of the Flood and merge with it. Sixteen cubits high, the final southern colossus of Ibshek thus represented the first image of the magical power of the ideal Flood, the one with the most beneficial spate.

The solar altar in the north of Meha was flanked by two small obelisks bearing four standing baboons adoring the sun. Against the wall to the north was a chapel; in the west, the statue of an immense scarab topped by the solar sphere (the image of Horakhty); in the east, an effigy of the seated baboon of Thoth capped by the lunar crescent (representing the Moon). The moon and the sun following one another, the loop is closed: this is eternity.

As dawn broke on New Year, and before starting home, Ramses would climb the few steps of the altar and, facing east, would conjure up the new sun between the two obelisks—thus vouchsafing the eternal recurrence of cyclical time.

Back to earthly realities

BEFORE THEY HEADED BACK to the delta, the stop-over at Thebes had given Ramses and the royal family an opportunity to explore the great court of the Temple of Luxor, which the royal architects were in the process of finishing. Colossi of the king, flanked by images of the Great Royal Wives (except for Isisnofret) had just been set up between each column encircling the court. Due to the close links they maintained with the royal *ka*, whose sanctuary it was, the three Great Wives were even permitted to enter the secret chambers of the temple,

The peace negotiations

IMMEDIATELY ON HIS RETURN TO Pi-Ramesse, Pharaoh learned of the arrival in the northern capital of some traveling Hittite noblemen who had established parley with the Bureau of Foreign

Facing page:
Colossus of
Ramses II.
Temple of Luxor.

Affairs. The slew of reports addressed to him by observers at the court of Hattusilis offered confirmation of the latter's maneuvers, designed both to protect him against the threat of machinations by the Assyrians and to defuse any potential aggression on the part of the Egyptians. It was judicious, then, to promote the idea of a relative relaxation in the Egyptian position with regard to their main adversary. Consequently, the two sovereigns settled on a compromise solution acceptable to both parties, who had much to gain from the agreement. Admittedly, Ramses had to jettison his dream of retaking Kadesh and holding sway over Amurru; on the other hand, it was now feasible for Egyptians to use the trade route that skirted the coast and ended at Ugarit, opposite Cyprus, without harassment. Egyptian protectorate over the entire area was reinforced, and the land of Kemi recovered the totality of its rights over the Phoenician ports. The Khatti would supervise Amurru, Upi would remain neutral, and Egypt would conserve its rights over Canaan. All this was understood tacitly; borders were not even mentioned.

Finally, an official peace treaty was signed between the Khatti and Egypt. It took almost two years of messengers flying back and forth between the two countries for the general lines of an agreement to be firmly laid down.

The peace treaty

The handing-over and appearance of the tablet

THE TEXT OF THE TREATY—the first in recorded history—was written in Babylonian, the diplomatic lingua franca of the time. In view of the expressions employed, it would seem to have been composed by lawyers in the service of Hattusilis, long familiar with the precise formulas of their country and with current practice. It had been drawn up, however, in collaboration with three eminent Egyptian men of law delegated by Pharaoh.

It comprises a large, very shiny silver tablet, engraved on both sides with cuneiform signs. In the center of the tablet, Ramses would have seen the Great Seal of the Hittite state: "The seal of Seth, sovereign of the sky, the seal of the treaty made by Hattusilis, the great master of the Khatti, the powerful son of Mursilis," and, on the reverse: "the seal of the Sun-goddess of Arinna, the sovereign of the country, the seal of Pudukhepa, the great sovereign of the country of the Khatti, daughter of the land of Kizzuwatna, priestess of the city of Arinna."

Peace treaty signed between Ramses II and the Hittite sovereign. Museum of Oriental Antiquities, Istanbul.

Ramses then summoned his scribe-interpreter to make an immediate translation of the treaty so it could be compared to the version in the Egyptian language which he already had at his disposal. After some minor modifications to the Babylonian text, copies on papyrus were lodged at the Bureau of Foreign Affairs, and the final version, again in Babylonian, was inscribed upon clay tablets; these were then handed over to a diplomatic mission commanded to present them to the Hittite sovereign Hattusilis in his palace of Hattusha. Lastly, Ramses gave orders that the ground-breaking document be engraved in Thebes—in hieroglyphs, naturally—on the walls of Karnak, and also in the Ramesseum, close to the scene of the battle of Kadesh. It also seems that another version was to appear on walls in the temples of Pi-Ramesse.

The content of the treaty

The treaty proposed first and foremost "Beautiful brotherhood and peace." It is, in its broad outlines, a pact enshrining mutual non-aggression, extradition, and humane treatment of those extradited,

Royal gate of Hattusha,
capital of the Hittites.
Boghazköy, Turkey.

as well as mutual assistance against attack. It treats finally of an alliance between the reigning families to ensure respect of the principle of legitimacy. Overall, its contents present features of international law still in force today.

While the Hittite and Egyptian versions do betray slight variants, in the overlapping section that is preserved, the two texts concur perfectly. Presenting a score or so paragraphs concerning the essential points, they refer several times to an agreement made with Egypt at the time when Suppiluliumas, a contemporary of the Amarna kings, ruled the Khatti. Very serious events had strained this convention to breaking point: prince Zananza, his son, whom the widow of Tutankhamun had thought of marrying, was assassinated on the road to Egypt, most probably on orders from Horemheb.

The Egyptian version of the treaty begins as follows: "The treaty that the great master of the Khatti, the hero, son of Mursilis, the great master of the Khatti, the hero, grandson of Suppiluliumas, the great master of the Khatti, the hero, has had written on a silver tablet for Usermaatre-Setepenre, great king of Egypt, the hero, son of Menmaatre, great king of Egypt, the hero: this honest treaty of brotherhood and peace, would that it offer peace and brotherhood between us, thanks to this treaty between the Khatti and Egypt, for all eternity! With regard to Muwatallis, the great master of the Khatti, he fought the great sovereign of Egypt. When he had succumbed to his fate,

Hattusilis took his place on the throne of his father. . . . Today, he has agreed by treaty to establish the relations Re has made between the land of Egypt and the land of the Khatti, to abandon hostilities between them forever. . . . Let the children of the great master of the Khatti remain in peace and brotherhood with the children of the children of Ramses. . . ."

Reference is then made in the main text to a non-aggression pact between the two sister nations, the renewal of the old treaty of entente signed under Muwatallis guaranteeing peace, the promise of joint defense were either to be attacked, as well as a commitment for Hattusilis' son to succeed his father under Egypt's wing. Last but not least, it addresses the question of extradition and amnesty of refugees, the latter to be imperatively returned to their country of origin without mistreatment.

The treaty finishes on the following note of warning: "With regard to the words engraved on this silver tablet of the land of the Khatti and the land of Egypt, the thousand divine forms of the land of the Khatti and the thousand divine forms of the land of Egypt will destroy the house, lands, and servants of any who fails to respect them. As for any who will respect the words inscribed on this silver tablet, Hittite or Egyptian, and who will take account of it, the thousand divine forms of the land of the Khatti and the thousand divine forms of the land of Egypt will ensure prosperity and life to him, his house, his country, and his servants."

Immediate consequences

RAMSES HAD BEEN GREATLY IMPRESSED by the imprint of the Hittite seal, for it contained the image of Seth protecting the Hittite king—Seth the patron of his family? And then, in another innovation, one of the faces of the official seal of the Hittite kingdom was dedicated to the queen, considered the equal of Hattusilis as "sovereign of the country." To show that he could be as "liberal" as the Hittites, Ramses wanted to emphasize how the women of his family also played an important part in affairs of state: Tuya and Nefertari were to become involved in these diplomatic exchanges and enter into correspondence with Queen Pudukhepa. Needless to say, Pharaoh received the famous tablet in silver—a metal that was extremely rare on the banks of the Nile—with great pomp and circumstance. The words of respect surrounding all mention of the names of both sovereigns testify to the reciprocal regard in which these rulers—"treating on an absolutely equal footing" and who

Hittite seals of Mursilis (top and photograph) and Tudliya IV, on which the king and queen appear.

already considered themselves as joint masters of the Middle East—held each other. And yet the attitude of the one-time antagonists could not have allowed them to meet, and it is uncertain whether they ever did, in spite of the links that would one day bind their families.

Nevertheless, festivities were held in both countries, and a courteous exchange of congratulations and an opening salvo of gifts were conveyed by couriers. Since, in the Hittite state, the queen shared in the highest responsibilities of the sovereign, in parallel with Hattusilis' letters to Ramses, Pudukhepa wrote to Nefertari, expressing her satisfaction in the fraternal peace that would henceforth reign between the two lands. To answer such a cordial overture, Nefertari summoned interpreters from the Ministry for Relations with Foreign Lands, who transcribed her response to Pudukhepa into Babylonian cuneiform.

The crown prince changes his name

THE QUEEN MOTHER, MUT-TUYA, in her turn likewise addressed missives of great nobility to the Hittite sovereigns, as, predictably, did Vizier Paser, since he had been instrumental in the preliminary exchanges of views that laid the foundations of the final treaty. Miraculously recovered, the archives of the Hittite capital contain, among many other items, the Egyptian crown prince's correspondence, though under a different name. No longer is it Imenherkhepeshef, but Sethherkhepeshef. Certain historians have jumped to the conclusion that the first must have passed away, but no document backs this up; moreover, this elder son of Ramses had already changed his name before. From Imenherwenemef, his name when he accompanied his father to war for the first time, by the end of the battle of Kadesh the little boy, thus protected under the aura of Amun, has become Imenherkhepseshef: ("He who receives his victorious weapon from Amun"). After the peace treaty, in which relations with the Khatti brought the empire of Ramses closer to that of another great land that venerated Seth, patron to the Khatti and to so many of her cities, it seemed expedient to replace the name of the senior son (that of the god of Thebes) with that of Seth, ancestor to the Ramesside *gens*. The crown prince was required to multiply contacts with his Hittite "father," and promptly wrote to the master of the Khatti, not only in congratulation, but also to inform him that he had "addressed gifts to [his] father through his envoy Parikhanawa."

News of the peace treaty was broadcast by the chancelleries, and official letters of notification were addressed to states with which the Khatti and Egypt maintained diplomatic relations. As the treaty endured, the situation thus created soon led to a resumption of relations between Egypt and Babylon: Ramses welcomed a Babylonian princess into his harem, while Hattusilis even managed to reach an accommodation with Salmanasar I of Assyria. And yet it took many years for the disagreement between Ramses and Hattusilis in connection with Urhi-Teshub, which was always bubbling away beneath the surface, to die down. The susceptibility of the Hittite had been irritated by the attitude of Pharaoh, who failed to apply the clause of the treaty stipulating the return of the unrepentant fugitive.

6

THE COMING
OF THE
GOD-KING

Facing page:
Erection of the djed *pillar by Pharaoh.*
Sanctuary of Osiris, Temple of Seti I, Abydos.

Death of the queen mother

IN THE TWENTY-THIRD YEAR of his reign, Ramses entered his forty-eighth year: he stood at the apogee of his power. He had recently made good a plan he had cherished since the battle of Kadesh and secured peace for his country. At all events, he had forged a crucial and, in the eyes of his neighbors, flattering entente with the most powerful adversary of the time. However, this "Sun of Egypt, who bends all foreign lands, the elect of Re in the barque of the Sun, the star of the sky, the sun of princes, the mountain of electrum and gold, the great one of victories, the perfect image of Re, the powerful bull, provider of Egypt. . . ." was now a man alone, broken, an orphan, for he had just lost a woman for whom he felt the deepest veneration, his mother, the great lady, Tuya.

In the Set-Neferu

THE SEPULCHER OF THE QUEEN mother in the Valley of the Queens had long been dug. It was the first in a row of rock chambers located on the western side of the wadi, with space for the burial of, first, immediately to the south, the queen mother, and then, proceeding northwards, Nefertari, followed by the daughters of Ramses, who in their turn had become Great Royal Wives, and finally the last of them, much loved by her grandmother, Hentmire.

The Valley of the Queens. Thebes.

The tomb of Tuya

A model of balance with very harmonious proportions, the tomb of Tuya comprised two underground levels, access to which was provided by a staircase cut into the limestone. The decorations were the main inspiration for the final dwelling-place of Nefertari, prepared shortly after that of Tuya. At the time I tracked down this "lost" tomb in the Valley of the Queens, the underground site was filled almost entirely with vestiges from several layers of tombs arranged in the openings, which had already been plundered for the first time before the end of the New Kingdom. Occasional ghosts of the reliefs flitted on the walls, silent witnesses to the glorious backdrop that had been prepared for the king's beloved mother. When, layer by layer, the site was emptied—a process that took several seasons of excavation—it was noted that this tomb, like all the other burial places of the Set-Neferu, had been built into very poor limestone. This particularity prevented artists from executing carvings, as was the case in the Valley of the Kings, on the excessively friable walls; instead, they would cover them with a layer of fine plaster upon which the décor was modeled prior to coloring.

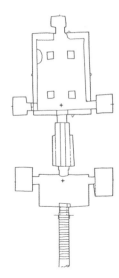

Plan of the tomb of Tuya.

The state of the tomb

The succession of tomb robbers who had destroyed the wall coating to defuse its magic power missed a few of the more resistant scraps. In the first room, one wall still bears relics of a large-scale decoration dominated by an image of the Theban peak. Elsewhere, a handful of divine figures can be made out. But, above all, there is the picture of the queen herself, in the form of a sphinx making an offering of ointment. One of the most significant discoveries in this tomb comes in the shape of the names and titles of the late incumbent, which in odd places on the walls remain readable: "Royal Mother Tuya." This brief description, accompanied by her titulary, is also mentioned on all the objects found in the tomb.

Anti-chamber, side-chambers

On the first level, the anteroom and annex on the left were above all to have featured canopic jars* containing the mummified internal organs and the funerary statuettes, the *shabtis* (*shawbtis*). Significant fragments made it possible for me to reconstitute three splendid canopic jars of the finest alabaster, with inscriptions in blue lapis-lazuli* paste in the name of the "Royal Mother Tuya." By chance, one of the four head-cum-lids of rare delicacy representing the figure of the queen was preserved. As for those on the remaining *shabtis*, often broken, in enameled light blue frit and of ritual simplicity, they were

Canopic jar: container used in Egypt for embalming organs.

Lapis-lazuli: rock best known as an ornamental stone, opaque and somewhere between azure blue and ultramarine in hue.

*Portrait of Queen Tuya
discovered in her tomb.
Lid from a canopic jar.
Luxor Museum.*

simply marked with the name of Tuya; under their feet, figures written in black ink showed that they had been numbered. The little room to the right on this first level seems to have been set aside for large and elegant earthenware vessels containing wine. Large fragments of these were recovered, bearing indications of their vintage, including one dated to the twenty-second year of Ramses' reign.

The funerary chamber

Spread out over the floor and benches in every room in this sepulcher was a treasure at least as rich as that of Tutankhamun. The second level consisted mainly of the funerary room, decorated with four pillars at the four points of the compass, in the center of which a large-size pink granite sarcophagus was to receive the mummy of the deceased, complete with its various gilded and/or pure gold sheaths. As prophylaxis, a quantity of jewels would have been inserted beneath the shroud and all along the linen strips or bandages, together with gold fingerstalls for the hands and cots for the feet. None of this magical apparatus has survived, save for fragments from the casket itself, cut out of the most beautiful pink granite of Aswan and covered with texts and geniuses of the Osirid family, incrusted as well as painted.

Highly precious objects and other materials necessary for the final transformation of the departed would have been placed around her. Evidence survives in the form of fragments of alabaster vessels, sometimes decorated with a floral relief, as well as others with the names of Seti, Ramses, and Nefertari. These jars and cups would certainly have contained the country's most exquisite ointments and most renowned perfumes. Other vessels are inscribed in ink on the belly with the names of the oils they contained. There were also small "make-up spoons"; one, intact and in alabaster, is carved into the shape of a duck with a hollow body.

One rather unexpected find comprised three significant fragments of a perfume jar made of perfectly transparent glass. Several other remnants of perfume pots were in opaque glass, made up of several superimposed layers of variously tinted paste wrapped around a mandrel. Still more evocative than these broken, but moving, relics is a fragmentary flask in frit originally shaped like a heart and inscribed with the name of the "Great Royal Wife," Bentanat. This daughter of Ramses and Isisnofret, then, must have been invested with a function in the twenty-second or twenty-third year of his reign, and not, as had hitherto been thought, in the thirty-eighth.

The opulence of Egypt

RAMSES WAS ALREADY SURROUNDED by dozens of children, most born to his secondary queens and concubines. Some had already died, as had a son of Nefertari's, Pareherwenemef. Shortly after, the king traveled to inspect work on his temple dedicated to Horakhty at Derr, in the land of Wawat, where he would have noted that the decorations were not quite finished. Few details have come down to us concerning the activities of the royal family between the twenty-third and twenty-sixth years of Ramses' reign; on the other hand, a mass of evidence speaks of the widespread wealth of the country, not to mention the riches piling up in the temple of Amun at Thebes. During the reign of the great pharaoh, the most talented officers of His Majesty's treasury, responsible for collecting taxes, but also, in exchange,

View of the ruins of the site of Deir el-Medineh. Thebes-West.

Statue of Panehsy, royal scribe and director of the treasury of Ramses II. British Museum, London.

for distributing proper salaries to the innumerable civil servants, were Panehsy and then Suty.

K. A. Kitchen has calculated that the revenue referred to in a letter by Panehsy to the priest of Amun, Hori, concerning the god's tenant farms in the delta, corresponds to one and three-quarter million bags of barley a year, roughly six million bovines, as well as goats; there were also one million game birds taken in the marshes of the delta. One then has to add eleven and a quarter million asses, and seven and a quarter million onagers (wild asses) captured. It should not be forgotten that this represents only part of the resources of the Temple of Amun to be distributed daily to the innumerable personnel employed there. Further additions would include the yield from the goldmines, naturally occurring electrum—found in large quantities in the land of Punt, though Egyptian chemists and metallurgists now knew how to manufacture it—as well as much other exotic produce, which Pharaoh would generously donate to the temple treasury to adorn liturgical furniture, plate or incrust the sacred boats and sanctuary doors, and so forth.

Two sons of Ramses

Shabti of Vizier Paser. Musée du Louvre, Paris.

AROUND THE TWENTY-FIFTH YEAR, the eldest son of Pharaoh was promoted to general-in-chief, a post he was to occupy until the fiftieth year of his father's reign (1254 to 1229 BCE). Meanwhile, Prince Meryatum, the king's sixteenth son, had recently been named high priest of Re at Heliopolis, a position he was to hold for the next twenty years.

Change of viceroy in Nubia

AT THE BEGINNING OF THE twenty-sixth year, a new viceroy of Nubia was appointed to replace Hekanakht. Ramses chose a certain Paser, the cousin of his dear friend Imeneminet, who had recommended him. Paser had visited his uncle, the commander of the troops in Nubia, Pennesuttawy, and his son and successor, Nakhtmin, in Wawat and the land of Kush, many times. Such individuals made for excellent informers, a crucial guarantee for Pharaoh. The new "governor" was to exercise his function in Nubia until the thirty-eighth year of Ramses' reign.

The death of the Great Royal Wife Nefertari

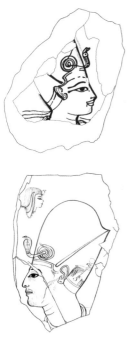

Above top: Ostracon *showing a pharaoh in mourning, drawn in a heavy line. Found at Deir el-Medineh. Musée du Louvre, Paris.*

Above bottom: Ostracon *illustrating the theme of pharaoh in mourning; here perhaps Ramses II. Found at Deir el-Medineh. Musée du Louvre, Paris.*

Above right: Ostracon *representing a Ramessid sovereign with sprouting beard. Musée du Louvre, Paris.*

ONCE AGAIN FATE WAS TO DEAL a cruel blow. The queen was wasting away. Neither the most famous *sinus* (doctors), whose reputation for knowledge had spread beyond Egypt's borders, nor the many foreigners consultants were able to diagnose her illness, still less cure it. Not even the chief physician to the residence of the queen, Khay, son of Huy, all of whose brothers numbered among the finest practitioners in the country, managed to save the sovereign. Nefertari-mery-Mut passed away, very probably in the twenty-sixth year. Following so close on one another, these two bereavements were stern reminders to Ramses that, although the incarnate son of god on earth, he was nonetheless a man of flesh and blood.

He had many times inspected the chamber destined for his beloved queen. The funeral lamentations were led by the chief mourners, daughters of the queen: Merytamun, Henuttawy, Baketmut, and Nefertari II. It was announced that Nefertari would journey to the celestial realm of the star and that none would replace her on earth. During the protracted preparation of the mummy, Ramses allowed his beard to grow as a sign of grief, as did the queen's sons: Sethherkhepeshef, the eldest, Sethemwia, Seti, Meryre, and Meryatum.

The tomb of the queen

The overall form of the rock tomb of Nefertari was borrowed from that of her mother-in-law, the queen dowager, close to whom she believed she would rest easy. As with the latter vault, however, this one, too, was violated and the funerary furniture plundered; even the mummy was torn apart in the ungodly search for gold and precious ointments. The tomb was found by an Italian mission at the beginning of the twentieth century, and the meager pickings it recovered are preserved in the Egyptian Museum of Turin. They constitute nevertheless the most beautiful and best preserved tombs from the Valley of the Queens, the walls presenting the most exceptional paintings known from the era. Bedecked with stars, the entire ceiling of the vault recalls the world beyond and the voyage to eternity. All around, the sovereign is greeted by elegant divinities who vie in nobility with Nefertari herself. In the vestibule, as the queen advances the pieces of the game of *senet* ("passing"), her opponent remains invisible because he represents, during the "purgatory" she has to cross, the ordeals and harmful agents that Nefertari must combat—and overcome—to attain bliss.

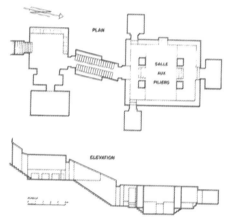

Below left: The mummy of Queen Nefertari on her funerary litter with the ibis and falcon. Tomb of Nefertari, Valley of the Queens, Thebes.

Below top: Undergoing the tests: the queen playing senet. Tomb of Nefertari, Valley of the Queens, Thebes.

Below bottom: Plan and section of the funerary vault of Nefertari.

Pages 170–171: General view of the funerary room of Nefertari: in the foreground, priests overseeing the rites; at the bottom, two of the four pillars adorned with djed that would watch over the mummy and its furniture. Valley of the Queens, Thebes.

The descent

The steep slope giving access to the funerary room is not, as in Tuya's vault, in the axis of the ante-room, but runs diagonally. On the walls of the descending shaft, the beautiful queen is seen making an offering of wine before the female form of Hathor, who prepares to welcome her into her bosom and to offer her rebirth in eternal life. Up to her ultimate transformation, Nefertari will be assisted by Anubis.

The vault

The second (lower) level of the vault consists of the ample chamber with four pillars, between which the large pink granite sarcophagus was lowered. Part of the décor represents two officiants wearing leopard skins, undoubtedly the two elder sons of the deceased, Sethherkhepeshef and Meryatum, preparing to welcome the mummy. Once the various coffin lids were closed, and that of the granite sarcophagus replaced, the fate of the deceased was entrusted to the four immense *djed* signs covering the inner faces of the pillars nearest to the outer sarcophagus.

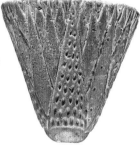

Isisnofret appears

WHETHER BY COINCIDENCE OR express intention, between the twenty-fourth and thirtieth years of Ramses' reign, images and references to Isisnofret, accompanied by her immediate family, start to appear in Upper Egypt. On a granite wall in the Aswan region, a rupestrian stele presents Ramses before Khnum, "Lord of the Cataract," accompanied by Isisnofret and Khaemwaset, then by Bentanat, her eldest daughter, General Ramses, her eldest son, and finally by the thirteenth son, and ultimate successor, Merenptah. Perhaps before this time she had occupied pride of place in the official decoration of the palace and temples of Memphis and at Pi-Ramesse, far from Thebes, but no vestige has survived in the greatly deteriorated ruins of the capital city. It does, however, seem that, following the death of Nefertari, a taboo was lifted. Shortly afterwards, another family group around the king and Isisnofret emerges: here, in Gebel Silsileh, Pharaoh is depicted making offerings of *maat* to Ptah. Before him is the priest-*setem*, Khaemwaset. The king is followed by Isisnofret and Bentanat. The lower register features the royal scribe and General Ramses, as well as the thirteenth son Merenptah. Nevertheless, such representations remain rare and sporadic. The children of Isisnofret, however, would stay faithful to her, in particular Khaemwaset, who was to raise monuments and

Above top: Amulet in the shape of the djed *pillar of Queen Nefertari. Museo Egiziano, Turin.*

Above bottom: Lotus flower in the name of "Queen Nefertari." Musée du Louvre, Paris.

Facing page: Detail: Nefertari presents the wine of divine ecstasy to Hathor; the passage from death to love. Tomb of Nefertari, Valley of the Queens, Thebes.

Above: *Ramses, Isisnofret, Khaemwaset. General Ramses, Princess Bentanat, and Prince Meneptah pay homage to Khonsu, lord of the Cataract. Rock-cut stele, Aswan.*

Above right: *Ramses offers maat to Ptah. He is preceded by Khaemwaset, followed by the Great Royal Wife, Isisnofret, and Princess Bentanat; with, on the lower register, General Ramses and Meneptah. Cave of Gebel Silsileh.*

ex-votos in her honor. At Sakkara and in the vicinity of the Serapeum, recently discovered architectural fragments allow one to suppose that a monument had been dedicated by the high priest of Ptah, Khaemwaset, to his venerated mother, Isisnofret.

An unresolved enigma

The absent queen reappeared, therefore, *once* Nefertari had passed away, but *not* after the death of the latter's eldest son. Why was she sidelined in this way? It is difficult to countenance that a perhaps understandable rivalry between the two Great Royal Wives might have influenced Ramses to such a degree, since his every public action, his every monument, was charged with significance. Until further information comes to light, it seems certain in any case that, prior to her demise, the stress had been placed on Nefertari, the queen who had given birth to the first son, and not on the first-born himself, who at the time was still only heir apparent. There is, moreover, a measure of ambiguity in the titles assigned to the first son that makes it hard to see exactly who was regarded as the chosen heir. One fact is undeniable: unlike his father Seti, Ramses apparently never appointed a co-regent.

It seems that a similar provision did not need apply to the second duo of Great Royal Wives, both admittedly daughters of Ramses:

Bentanat and Merytamun. They are found, for instance, represented strictly in parallel on two colossi of the king from the Temple of Herakleopolis. If Isisnofret were still alive at this time, she had become queen dowager.

A new high priest of Amun

R AMSES WAS DETERMINED TO relieve the brilliant Vizier Paser from the countless offices he had accumulated during the reign. The death of the high priest of Amun, the First Prophet Wennofer, father of Imeneminet, presented an opportunity to propose the pontificate to the best viziers. Before relinquishing his functions in the twenty-seventh year of the reign, Paser once again inspected the team of workmen engaged on the royal necropolises, whom he had always supervised. He took part in the final "Beautiful Festival of the Valley," celebrated under his authority in the second month of summer. During the procession, he accompanied with devotion the divine

During the "Beautiful Festival of the Valley," Ramses wafts incense over the barque of Amun, followed by the vizier, Paser.

barque, which traveled to the Ramesseum before being deposited in the hypostyle hall. There it was greeted by Ramses himself, wafting incense over the sacred vessel of Amun, the *Userhet*, at its mooring in the jubilee temple. Then Paser took the road which leads from the western plain at the foot of the *gebel* through a dried-out wadi and on towards that of the "Great Field". At a junction with a secondary wadi, the "Valley of the Monkeys" (Gabbanet el-Gonsud), also known as the "Valley of the West", he chose a rock bordering the road and had engraved upon it two graffiti addressed to the goddess Hathor, patron of the necropolis and guarantor of solar rebirth, in which he sought to ratify the protection granted postmortem to his master for his eternal dwelling-place, on which he had toiled so tirelessly.

Home affairs: Ramses applies the *maat*

To succeed, after a fashion, the irreplaceable Paser, who had, with him, practically fashioned the kingdom, Ramses called upon Khay to be inducted as southern and northern vizier. This marked the beginning of a time when external peace and wealth at home left the field free for a measure of cupidity, readily detectable in the behavior of some of the senior officials supervising the goods amassed in the royal temples and warehouses.

During the twenty-eighth and twenty-ninth years of Ramses' reign, a veritable scandal erupted in the western area of Thebes, exposed by Hatia. For some time, the scrupulous scribe had been patiently observing the machinations of a lady who, on the slightest pretext, would visit a royal storehouse on the left bank and "cream off" the contents. He finally decided to lodge a complaint with a tribunal, which opened a preliminary investigation and soon discovered that the woman was the wife of the wealthy individual in charge of stores containing goods belonging to several temples of the left bank. There arose the suspicion, and then the certitude, that this notable individual had rarely resisted the temptation to remove "samples" from the treasure he was entrusted to defend. Enjoying the total confidence of the new vizier, he had been promoted as Inspector of the Herds in the north of the delta. Even on the departure of its "herdsman," however, the milch-cow proved too alluring to be left in peace, and the wife and daughter continued their pilfering in the name of a paterfamilias who no longer even had responsibility over the warehouse.

Pharaoh, ever watchful over his entire territory, was alerted at once, since there could be no question of hushing up such a grievous misdeed. The business was treated very seriously, for if Ramses did not react rapidly and with the utmost rigor to such events, other cases would be sure to come about, sowing disorder in the country and destabilizing what was called *maat*—the balance Pharaoh was meant to guarantee and for which he must make regular offerings to the creator. He thus appointed the crown prince himself, now named Sethherkhepeshef, aided and abetted by a number of high-ranking dignitaries, to chair the High Court before which the long-fingered matron was subpoenaed. The investigation revealed that the thefts committed by the two women and by the functionary prior to his promotion had been considerable: 20,000 bushels of grain, divers quadrupeds, including 30 bulls and 10 goats, as well as 30 geese; 30 chariots with equipment, 1,300 bits of copper ore, 424 pieces of linen clothing, 440 leather sandals, and wine-jars of various vintages. When summoned to the court, other larcenies were laid at the door of the new Inspector of the Herds of the delta. Bad faith and cynicism seemed to have been this man's life blood, and, though presented with indisputable proof of his misdeeds, he rejected it haughtily. Loudly protesting his innocence, he did not shrink from solemnly swearing before the assessors and the jury so as to divert the blame on the guards and accuse them of the misappropriation with which he was inculpated.

The end of the story has unfortunately not come down to us. It is however probable that the trial was an expeditious one, since Pharaoh was keen to repress with vigor and speed dereliction in any of the empire's fundamental institutions. There must have been many arrests, because one cannot without witnesses or accomplices spirit away such a quantity of objects including chariots, bulls, etc. The arrests and the severe penalties would not have been limited to three members of an errant family.

Foreign affairs: the beginning of a friendship

For Egypt, the alliance with the Khatti had, without doubt, afforded interior stability and a remarkable measure of security in its relations with foreign countries, a situation Ramses strove to maintain with vigor and vigilance. It was now widely realized that to attack Egypt meant to incur a reaction on the part of the Khatti, anxious to honor the treaty and keep their word.

Whether the harmony between the great powers was quite so idyllic remains an open question. Exchanges started between Egypt and the Khatti on a commercial level; then, thanks to these initial contacts, the Hittites called upon the science of the Egyptians

(medicine, pharmacopoeia) and were soon appreciating the linen, marvelous weaving, and elegant jewelry they produced. Egypt, for its part, possessed relatively meager iron mines, whereas the province of Kizzuwatna, whence Queen Pudukhepa originated, boasted a thriving industry in this sector. This metal was essential to Pharaoh for modernizing his troops, who had to be equipped with solid rapiers, helmets, and armor (such as breastplates) capable of confronting the weapons of those tribes—the future "invaders from the sea"—against whom, for the moment, the Hittites formed a bastion. It was also necessary to keep Pharaoh's great strength uppermost in the minds of the Assyrians.

With regard to the attitude of the two former antagonists, surviving documents imply that Ramses had not been able to throw off the cavalier attitude with which he had so often treated the smaller states of the Near East. It transpires from the tone of certain missives found in the correspondence between the sovereigns that Hattusilis had on occasion to pull Pharaoh up. The Egyptian, keen not to rock the boat, would answer with flattering terms and professions of faith, in the hope of sweeping his *faux pas* under the carpet. The correspondence as a whole betrays the great differences in character between the two sovereigns; the wise, patient, peace-loving Hattusilis, and the hotheaded and tempestuous, but also mystical and skilful, Ramses. Over time, however, and with growing experience of each other, they managed to present an image of concord and peace.

The first jubilee of the thirtieth year

I N THE TWENTY-NINTH YEAR of his reign, the whole of Egypt was preparing to pay homage to Pharaoh. The great *sed* ceremony had to be imperatively celebrated during the thirtieth year of rule. Certainly, the festivals of New Year's Day already made an annual contribution to sustaining the inheritance Pharaoh owed to the divine impulse that underpinned his royal power.

When the time of the great thirty-year feast arrived, afterwards to be repeated every three years, Pharaoh was to undergo various trials to enter the stage of total incorporation with the master of life (Osiris), in order to rule on the throne of the living. As with all ceremonies involving secret rituals, the documents which might have thrown light on them are peppered with allusions that are hard to interpret, and, to date, it has proved impossible to provide an accurate reconstitution of the ceremonial. Little else can be done but analyze certain depictions that provide but a pale reflection of the events.

For the festival, Ramses had an immense and lavishly decorated hall built at Pi-Ramesse. In all probability, the reliefs adorning the walls of the surrounding chapels would have referred to the overall aspect of the mysteries. It is known that the ceremonies and festivities were prepared a full year in advance and lasted an entire Nile cycle. This jubilee (or *sed* festival) was to be officially "proclaimed" by the highest sacerdotal authorities in the land involved with this particular ritual, and by the head of government. Thus it was that Prince Khaemwaset, high priest of Ptah, master of the jubilees, and the new vizier, Khay, announced the event. The whole country was mobilized, and while the essential religious ceremonies were held for Pharaoh at Pi-Ramesse and then at Memphis, they were also celebrated in Nubia, in the temples at Abu Simbel and Aksha. The exploitation of the "miraculous" that Ramses was so adroit at turning to his advantage, and which appeared repeatedly throughout his life, resurfaces once again on the occasion of his first thirty-year anniversary, which was duly a providentially "good year."

Glimpses of life at Pi-Ramesse

Now transpires the extent to which Hathor, the great mistress by whose bosom any candidate to renewal must pass, played, in the general scheme of things, an essential role for Ramses, as for his chief wife. Nefertari having left this earth, a question arose. Was Isisnofret, mother of Khaemwaset, the director of the jubilee, to take on the role of Hathor, and Bentanat that of Sothis, next to the king? Or would the second generation of Great Royal Wives, Bentanat and Merytamun,

Following pages: *King Ramses II receiving the jubilee hieroglyphics from the god Amun-Re. Great Temple of Amun, Karnak.*

Departure of the royal
couple on the barque of
the night. On the lower
register, ritual dances
by the women of the Oases.
Pi-Ramesse, Qantir.

play the part of the two goddesses flanking His Majesty, enthroned at the beginning of the festivities?

Ramses appeared at the door to his palace. Among the brilliant retinue of dignitaries also appeared members of the "crew of the barque," for part of the ceremony was to take place on the lake at the residence, mainly during the night. Dancers and musicians then executed a rhythmical performance, accompanied by all sorts of acrobatic and choreographic mummery. Chants rose into the air on this "day to exalt what must be exalted," with female musicians intoning the anthem for Hathor.

When, accompanied by the queen, the king strode out of the palace, he wore the short skirt of the jubilee that left the knees free. After the ceremony of "Mooring the boat to the night," the sovereign took part in the procession on water, a kind of ritual sailing trip. Then the princesses of the royal family would enter, playing the *sistrum* with the female choir of Amun. All the officiants accompanied the royal couple as they took their seat in the barque of the night, marking the beginning of the symbolic voyage, a nautical cortège that had to take place to coincide with the arrival of the "Great Nile": the Flood (*Hapy-aa*). The geniuses of the jubilee were also loaded on to the boat. At dawn, the "opening of the mouth"—the act that gives back life—was performed on the solar barque and accompanied by offerings of cattle and other livestock.

The pivotal rite at Memphis

It seems that, for Pharaoh, one of the final chapters in the mystery of the great jubilee ceremonial consisted in erecting the *djed* pillar, the paramount emblem of Osiris at the time of his resurrection. The scene was to take place south of Giza, in the *shetyt* (or *shetat*) of the god Sokar (Seker). At dawn, Ramses, followed by the Great Royal Wife and the princesses, the mysterious *setem* priest, and the Chief of the House of Craftsmen, himself proceeded to set up the *djed* pillar representing the *ka*. The princesses were also expected to present sacred objects to induce renewal by the action of the beautiful Hathor. The ritual dance was now given rhythm by a hymn intoned by a male chorus, while Ramses, holding ropes attached to a great *djed* pillar, slowly raised this emblem of the cycle pertaining to all four cardinal points of the ordered world. Then the "double doors of the subterranean world opened" for Osiris-Sokar.

This image of the majestic *djed* pillar, this *ka* which dwells in the House of Sokar, was also Ptah-Sokar, amalgamated with Pharaoh as his virility revived: the ageing of darkness was driven out and replaced by a shining light. As the symbolic pillar was being hoisted into position, men armed with great papyrus stems set to with their marshy weapons, simulating the battle between opposing forces. They were meant to strike hard, but, in the end, order was restored, and it was proclaimed: "Horus appearing in truth has overcome."

Then the divine Fathers were again to receive nourishment in their barque, while one final devotion during the ceremony of the erection of the *djed* was evoked by a procession of cattle and a herd of

Bottom: *In Memphis, Pharaoh accompanied by the queen re-erects the* djed *pillar. The royal princesses play the* sistrum. *Memphis.*

Below: *Ritual cup containing the image of the sovereign "renewed" by the two sacred plants. Memphis.*

asses. The *djed* pillar was always kept in the House of Sokar, who vouched for the success of the ceremony, and was tended and continuously honored with offerings until the following jubilee.

The king and the "primeval mothers"

The ceremonies at Pi-Ramesse would have concluded with one last symbolic offering, probably presented to the royal couple. This last ritual might also have been performed by Khaemwaset himself for his father at the great Temple of Ptah at Memphis, which also housed a large jubilee building, and the hypostyle hall, which served as the counterpart to one in the Temple of a Million Years in the Ramesseum. For this ultimate ceremony, Ramses sat next to the Great Royal Wife under the double platform of rebirth. The sovereign was offered tributes in the form of symbolic objects of gold-work, the crucial element being a cup whose bowl was reminiscent of a lotus bloom and whose side-handles were carved in the shape of ibex heads. Surprisingly, the top of this object features a bucolic scene, in the center of which a tiny image of Ramses stands out before a bush of "lilies" and papyrus. With one hand, the king holds against his chest three papyrus stems, while with the other he grasps before him three stems of "lily." This highly original composition should be seen as a supremely poetic allusion to the pool of primeval water. The dominant ornament is, in point of fact, the scene engraved on the inside, which depicts the royal solar child being reborn to his new earthly life once the jubilee rites have been accomplished. The entire Egyptian population was drawn into the performance of certain public episodes of the ceremony, while, in the enclosure of the capital Pi-Ramesse, representatives of vassal allies attended the unfolding mystery.

Pharaoh's new lease of life

THE RESTORED VIGOR ONCE AGAIN, if temporarily, circulating in Ramses' veins was to provide fresh impetus to his extraordinary existence. Peace now reigned in the Near East; the alliance between the two great contracting powers continued unabated, but Ramses' aims were loftier still, and he had started to dream of a union that might cement his links with the Hittite royal family and thereby reinforce the image of his power. However, the heiress to Hattusilis and Pudukhepa could not be compared to the minor princesses of the Near East, all too flattered to enter the harem of Pharaoh as a show of submission. The proud and noble Hattusilis had, moreover, never aired such a transaction. In addition, Ramses was regularly updated as to progress on the underground workings he had started on again, at least from the nineteenth year of his reign, in the Valley of the Kings. Outside the entrance to his own rock-cut tomb he had decided to dig out immense subterranean apartments, a kind of multi-cell tomb-cenotaph dedicated to his innumerable sons and grandsons.

As usual, Ramses wished to be kept informed of every detail of life in his lands, even those relating to the payment of the workmen and craftsmen employed on the royal necropolises. He thus received, some time around his jubilee year (the thirtieth or thirty-first year of his reign), a message from his chief of the treasury, Suty, a royal scribe, informing him through the vizier Khay of the quality and quantity of the food served to the "Workmen on the Tomb" for the entire year.

Meha hit by an earth tremor

AROUND THE THIRTY-FIRST YEAR of his reign, Ramses was informed that the region of Thebes had suffered a number of seismic upheavals. Shortly afterwards, Vizier Khay, followed by the viceroy of Nubia, Paser, alerted His Majesty that his favorite temple,

Aerial view of the Valley of the Kings.

the great *speos* of Abu Simbel, had been spectacularly affected. Ramses immediately set off to the south to inspect the extent of the damage for himself. Close to the entrance door, the first southern colossus had suffered grievously, with the torso and head lying dashed to pieces on the ground. Moreover, the right arm of the first northern colossus seemed likely to fall at any moment. Inside the great court, the second north Osirid pillar displayed deep cracks and the two southern pillars were on the point of collapse.

Orders were immediately issued to Viceroy Paser, responsible for overseeing the works, to erect scaffolding and repair the damage as well as he might. The friable character of the sandstone, however, made it impossible to replace and finish the upper reaches of the colossus on the frontage, so it was left where it lay. The earth had trembled, and the shock that had damaged the entrance to the *speos* had surely arisen in the province of Ptah—lord of the jubilees, in his form as *Ta-tenen*: "The Earth that rises up"! Ramses at once made a vow to dedicate a long address to the master of Memphis, without missing the opportunity to indulge in some self-praise and turn the catastrophe into a good augury. This text would cover the lower, bracing wall between the two southern Osirid pillars in the great court.

Ramses' intrigues

RAMSES' ENVOYS' COVERT OPERATIONS aimed at Hattusilis and his entourage had had their effect—all the more so as the Khatti were going through a series of ordeals, including an unusual and worryingly persistent drought. On his return to the capital of the north, Pharaoh received some highly gratifying news from his advisors, that gave succor to a long-cherished project: to marry Hattusilis's eldest daughter and elevate her, exceptionally, to the status of Great Royal Wife. But the proposal itself had to come from Hattusilis. In the meantime, the whole of Egypt was soon busy celebrating the sumptuous festivals of his second jubilee, which were to extend throughout the thirty-third year of his reign.

Engagement proposals

DURING THE YEAR OF THE SECOND JUBILEE, as proclaimed once again by Khaemwaset and Vizier Khay, towards the end of the Flood, the long-awaited initiative took shape: Hattusilis dispatched messages to Ramses in which he proposed the union to Pharaoh in the spirit of strengthening the alliance between the two countries. Once the customary enthusiasm and congratulations had been run through, the exchange of letters broached the question of practical realization. Did Ramses condescend to let it be known that he would accept a dowry worthy of his grandeur, or did the Hittite spontaneously open the subject so as to win over Pharaoh, whose support he was now on the brink of obtaining? Whatever happened, an epistle from Hattusilis still exists in which he announces the splendid dowry to be granted his daughter and his wish that Pharaoh prepare an escort to receive it. Ramses eagerly replied that the escort would be secured as far as Egypt.

Isisnofret and the second jubilee

FOR THE ARRIVAL OF THE FLOOD and the second jubilee, the rise of the waters was sanctioned by inscriptions at Gebel Silsileh. Once again, Isisnofret, the Great Royal Wife, appeared on a rock stele escorting Pharaoh and accompanied by the three elder sons she had given the king. The other new Great Royal Wife, the beautiful Merytamun, daughter of Nefertari, did not take part in the ceremony. She seems, for all that, to have remained close to the king; but at Gebel Silsileh, pride of place went to the nuclear family of Isisnofret, even though the heir to the crown, the son of Nefertari, Sethherkhepeshef, was still alive. Isisnofret had not been present at the Nubian great mysteries. Now that Nefertari had passed away, her place was to be taken by the other principal Great Royal Wife still on the scene, at the time of the rites dedicated to the Nile for her happy arrival in the land of Kemi. She seems, though, to have been condemned to remain in obscurity during the more glorious hours of Ramses' reign: none of the official documents found to date—in particular, the correspondence exchanged between the two courts concerning the peace treaty—refer to the queen or mention the name Isisnofret. However, at a later date, Khaemwaset and General Ramses, her two elder sons, both erected monuments to her in Memphis.

Ramses goes too far in his demands

NEWS FROM THE KHATTI petered out, and Ramses expressed his astonishment at the delay in "negotiations" and his misgivings regarding a dowry he felt should be a substantial one—as he had been promised. Doubtless to avoid muddying the waters between such powerful potentates, the Hittite answer came via Queen Pudukhepa. From her reply to Ramses it transpires that the subjects broached by the latter included a claim that he was in need of the agreed dowry in order to "balance his budget"! The queen's sharp reaction employed unambiguous terms and pointed arguments: "That you, my brother, wish to grow rich at my cost . . . is neither fraternal, nor to your honor. . . ." During what amounted to a dressing-down, Pudukhepa also seized the opportunity to reproach Ramses for failing in respect of a clause in the peace treaty, since he had never agreed to return to his native land the fugitive Urhi-Teshub, as Hattusilis had requested. Obviously, this placed the recipient in an awkward situation. Thus are enduring family bonds forged! The whole issue soon blew over, however, and apparently in a rather unexpected fashion. Ramses was careful not to waste any more time and quickly dispatched a delegation to ritually anoint the princess with the fine oils much vaunted by Egypt's neighbors. The rite most probably occurred at the beginning of the *shemu* (dry season) in the year 1246 BCE. As Pudukhepa solemnly declared: "Fine oil was poured onto the head of [my] daughter, [then] the gods of hell were driven away. On that day, the two great countries became one land, and you, the two great kings, discovered true brotherhood."

Ramses and his capital await the princess

THE MARVELOUS CITY OF Pi-Ramesse prepared to receive the princess, a beauty among beauties. Building work at Pi-Ramesse hardly stopped for breath. Following a carefully devised urban plan, the headquarters of the civil and military administration were arranged around the royal palace. Admittedly, the city of Memphis, with its arsenals, barracks, and docks (Peru-Nefer), remained the focus of power; but Pi-Ramesse doubled these installations around the palace and temples at the four cardinal points. They were surrounded by barracks; dwellings for the senior officials and the princely residence of Paser in the north were located not far from the sanctuaries of Ptah and Sekhmet. Close by the great ceremonial space set up at the time of the first jubilee in the thirtieth year of Ramses' reign featured a forecourt decorated with six granite obelisks. The large hall, with its central columns measuring twenty feet (six meters) in height recalled, albeit in less impressive proportions, the immense hypostyle hall at Karnak. The number of colossi of Pharaoh, their gigantic scale embodying the royal function made divine, increased steadily. Residences earmarked for the use of the future Great Royal Wife and for her retinue were under construction. The princess's residence would be laid out in sophisticated apartments, with walls decorated with paintings depicting nature at her most graceful; the flagstones imitated flower beds, and there were pictures of pools dotted with lotus plants and beneficent fish with gleaming scales gliding past.

Terraces provided with elegant loggias commanded a view onto the distant lake, a wide part of the "Waters of Avaris" that ran round the city, flowing from the branch of the Nile known as the "Waters of Re." The garden was hastily planted so that the eyes of the princess might be charmed by spring blossoms. Hollyhocks, tufts of chamomile, poppies, and cornflowers imported from Canaan and Amurru were laid, though papyrus and lotus more typical of Egypt already graced the avenues and ponds; not far off, vine arbors, sycamores, date-palms and persea had been picked out into the rich humus.

The lavish materials from the warehouse stores now being crafted into luxury goods of the highest quality were simply unbelievable. Armchairs, seats, and clothing-trunks by the most talented cabinet-makers of Nubia, for instance, or elaborate goldwork. Near the palace, glassmakers prepared jars; for ointments, for the choicest perfumes, and for eye make-up, the craftsmen would cast a colored, or even transparent, crystalline paste. The products of the land of Punt would spread throughout the princely apartments; intricate goldwork confections would decorate plinths in the reception halls.

Finally, the princess's private apartments were given a finishing touch with a dressing-room in which bolts of gossamer-like linen

Following pages: Painting of the New Kingdom representing an Egyptian garden. British Museum, London.

Fragments of decoration from a palace at Qantir, Pi-Ramesse.

awaited her, together with pleated dresses with batwing sleeves adorned with brightly colored woven belts, sometimes embellished with the tiniest pearls. The trousseau was designed to introduce the princess to Egyptian fashions, more elegant and less ponderous than that of Anatolia with its less clement climate. Tall boxes with a wooden "mushroom" stand in the center were hung with various elaborately constructed wigs of natural hair, each destined for a particular special occasion. Alabaster vases of Hatnub kept floral essences fresh and were deposited in the anointing room next to another set aside for perfume showers and fitted with a device providing flowing water similar to that in the sanitary facilities close by.

Everything was sure to be ready for the young Khatti princess when she reached the end of her long journey.

Cosmetic jar. Egyptian Museum, Cairo.

An exceptional marriage

THE CHRONICLE RELATING THE VOYAGE of the Hittite bride-to-be from her capital of Hattusha in Anatolia to her arrival in Ramses' presence at his palace of Pi-Ramesse was inscribed by order of His Majesty in Abu Simbel, on a large stele set aside in the rock of Meha, south of the terrace of the *speos*.

In an extraordinary tour de force, the distant memory of the battle of Kadesh, which had weighed so heavily later on the conduct of the king and had governed his acts on the military and diplomatic front for so long, now dissolved into Ramses' union with the daughter of his ancient and very powerful adversary. It was a turnaround that surely constituted the culmination of his reign. Pharaoh had the same text engraved, more or less abridged, in the temple of Karnak, on Elephantine and in Upper Nubia, in the temples of Aksha and Amara-west.

Various toilet requisites: pot and shell with kohl, stylet, and pin. Musée du Louvre, Paris.

Was Hattusilis' arm twisted perhaps?

Certain passages on this stele, admittedly particularly difficult to decipher, seem to suggest that the Hittite king, reeling from some disaster, had consulted with his officers and finally agreed to make significant gifts to Ramses, the chief of these being his eldest daughter. The text, however, also brings out how Ramses could hardly conceal his joy at the announcement of a decision that crowned all his stratagems with success.

The route followed by the princess

The itinerary for the princess's lengthy journey was surely reconnoitered by scouts, leveled by sappers to render the defiles in the mountain and roads less arduous, and parceled out by military relays. As a result, communications between the two countries subsequently became much easier.

After leaving Hattusha, the future Maathorneferure and her sumptuous procession probably made for Kadish, to the southeast, before proceeding due south, through the defiles of Taurus and towards Adana, passing by Kizzuwadna before reaching Aleppo, and finally Kadesh on the Orontes. After accompanying her to the southernmost limits of the country of Amurru, Queen Pudukhepa bid farewell to her daughter on the fringes of the Pi-Ramesse of Canaan, on the borders of Temesq (Damascus).

Drawing of the wedding scene. The princess, accompanied by Hattusilis, advances towards the throne room where Ramses sits enthroned with Seth and Ptah-Tenen. Abu Simbel.

Explanation of the second marvel

This fantastic adventure was until very recently enveloped in obscurity. It had been thought that, at a certain juncture in the voyage, Seth, master of the dynasty, in an effort to protect the beautiful traveler—and indubitably the emissaries dispatched by Pharaoh to meet her—from the inconveniences of rain, cold, and snow, had, at Ramses' request, performed one of the "miracles" the king was apt to employ,

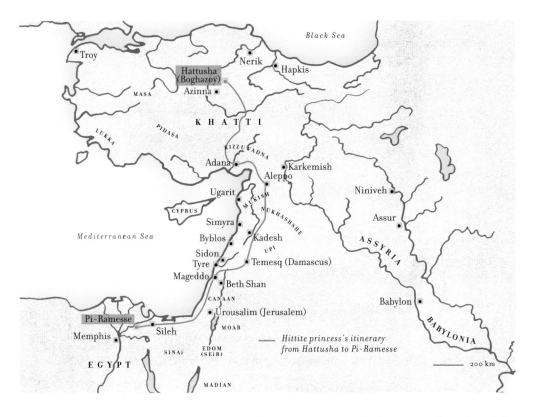

The Hittite princess's route from Hattusha to Pi-Ramesse.

and a sudden bout of summery weather had temporarily replaced the rigors of the Syrian winter.

In point of fact, Ramses, ever the astute politician ready to turn any and every event to his advantage, had made the most of what is known as "Saint Martin's Summer," a phenomenon with which his astronomers and geographers were well acquainted, and had taken the credit for yet another "miracle."

The first wonder

On the other hand, a fresh study of the text militates in favor of the existence of *two* "miracles" occasioned by Ramses, and reveals an earlier event which would provide a motive for that sudden U-turn in Hattusilis' attitude with respect to Ramses we noted above.

The Khatti, as has been mentioned, were going through an extremely arid period, prolonged by abnormal warmth at the beginning of winter that threatened to make the country—after years of hostilities—dependent on Egypt. These serious climatic disturbances would have been used by Pharaoh to pressurize Hattusilis and force him to accede to his requests. With Ramses' demands met, Seth no longer felt the urge to vent his anger on the Hittite. He thus restored the seasons to their rightful place, and the drought promptly broke: the princess could then start out to Egypt under more normal skies. Ramses had performed a first miracle.

It was now that the second miracle took place. Ramses had sent a delegation to meet the princess: making the most of the imminent appearance of the "Saint Martin's Summer," he proclaimed loudly that he found it unacceptable that his delegates were to suffer the rigors of a climate to which they were not accustomed, and passed the word that Seth had intervened once again, this time against the inclement weather, so that "summer days occur in winter."

Maathorneferure, Great Royal Wife

I N THE THIRD MONTH OF THE *peret* season of the thirty-fourth year of her extraordinary fiancé's reign, the Hittite princess, with great pomp and circumstance, was conducted to the palace of Ramses and into the presence of the sovereigns and foreign vassals. She was baptized with an Egyptian name immediately recorded on monuments prepared in the interval before she arrived. She became Maat-Hor-Neferu-Re ("She-who-sees-Horus-the-Incarnation-of-Re"). In spite of the degraded state of the stone, at the summit of the great marriage stele carved at Abu Simbel, Pharaoh can still be made out beneath the dais of the great audience chamber of the palace, flanked by two divine forms, those who performed his miracles: Seth and Ptah.

The princess is represented walking towards him, followed by her father, Hattusilis, and the inscription engraved in front of her declares that she is the daughter of the great king of the Khatti. There is, however, no documentary evidence to indicate that Hattusilis did in fact personally present his daughter to Ramses in this way. The texts mention only that Pudukhepa accompanied the princess to the limit of the zones of influence of the two lands.

Scarabs in the name of Maathorneferure were issued; as was the fashion at that time, poets dedicated tributes in the form of three-dimensional rebuses to her, as well as amulets made up of the cryptograms employed to write her Egyptian denomination, but there is little evidence concerning her as an individual, and her Hittite name is not known. Emerging from the gloom, however, the Boghazköy archives contain copies of a letter Hattusilis addressed to Ramses after the news the latter had sent to his "pal" concerning a grand-daughter Maathorneferure had recently brought into the world. The response of Hattusilis is revealing: "It's a pity that it is not a son; I would have willingly kept my throne warm for him."

The Blessing of Ptah

Thus, the hymen of Ramses and Maathorneferure had been blessed by Seth, but also by Ptah-Tenen. It was perhaps partly for this reason that the great inscription at Abu Simbel (nowadays called the "Blessing of Ptah") was engraved.

The climax of the text consisted in an allusion to another incredible miracle, one announced three years before: the arrival of Maathorneferure at Pi-Ramesse, in February of the thirty-fourth year of Ramses' reign. Roughly nine months after the wedding, in the first month of the second season, in the thirty-fifth year, on the thirteenth day, this date might coincide with the birth of an Egyptian descendant to the great king of the Hittites, an event of the greatest importance, we can be sure. It seems that, following a custom current in Egypt, the name of the newborn princess was formed on that of her mother, Neferure.

An earthquake, a portent

All this stemmed from the "wonder." The earthquake that had seriously shaken the front section of the great *speos* of Meha in the thirty-first year had provided Ramses with yet another unmissable opportunity in his climb to complete deification.

With a fantastic flair for timing and an exacerbated attraction for symbols, he transformed the recent catastrophe into a blessing and a premonitory message. He had, at the appropriate juncture, turned to Seth to bring a perilous drought to the Hittite; then, having forced Hattusilis to accede to his demands, had further obtained from his patron god the return of winter to the land of the Hittite. Now came the time to stress the action of Ptah-Tatenen, "the earth that rises up," reigning over the telluric forces, and present in the foundations of Meha, in the shadows at the rear of the sanctuary.

Yet another miracle

Henceforth, Ramses was to place himself under the aegis of the great master of the jubilees, and join to his Horus name the epithet of "Lord of the *sed* festivals like his father Ptah-Tenen." The earthquake, having made his temple of predilection shudder, and disfigured one of the colossi on the frontage, might have been interpreted as a repudiation, a curse even, on the person of Pharaoh, but the opposite was the case.

The point was to show that the earth had trembled as a sign of divine favor, and to announce a future wonder: the union with the daughter of his old and still redoubtable adversary, so as to win, at last, "his" battle of Kadesh! This much-deserved, but still inaccessible intervention could only proceed from a father from whom he had earned a state of grace in the period shortly after his first two *sed* festivals. He was, then, to return to a theme already exploited in the marriage stele, but, on this occasion, for a veritable dialog with he who was about to become his father: Ptah-Tenen.

The bracing wall in the great temple of Meha, erected between the two southern Osirid pillars in the great court, was now inscribed with a long hieroglyphic text, a version of which was also discovered in the temple of Aksha. From the very outset, the king's divine procreation is made clear. In this new stage of the royal existence, Ptah-Tenen has supplanted Amun. The legitimacy of his power has been given him again by Ptah; Sekhmet, the female counterpart to the master of the jubilees, is referred to as his mother.

Ramses in the divine family

The inscription, of course, records all the benefits that will accrue to Ramses and his country: happiness, wisdom, and power, as well as agricultural, mining, and industrial wealth; but the crucial point was to recall that, if the marriage with the Hittite princess occurred at all, it was because the god had acted to that purpose and had so informed his son: "I caused the earth shocks for you to announce the great sacred miracle to you; the sky trembled, and those present were gladdened by what befell you. The mountains, the waters, and the walls which are on earth were shaken because they saw the edict I decreed for you. . . . The people of the Khatti will be serfs in your palace. . . . This I placed in their hearts to bring them bowing before your *ka*, the tributes of their chief and their gifts to the power of Your Majesty, and his [eldest] daughter at their head. . . ."

In response to such favors, which should be recognized as the culmination of the reign, Ramses had to ensure Ptah-Tatenen of his immense filial devotion, so explaining the description of the many foundations dedicated to his father in Memphis. The great Memphite temple of Ptah still presents ruins that speak of its size and annexes, as well as of the chapel erected to associated divine entities, such as Hathor, "Lady-of-the-southern-sycamore." The triumphal avenues are still marked out by ruins of pylons and monumental statues. A number of likenesses of the king have been exhumed from the palm plantation of Memphis, including the large prone colossus, an uncontested masterpiece of Ramesside art, as well as the very famous statue of Ramses now preserved in the Museo Egiziano of Turin.

Those great royal ladies

THE EXACT ROLES ENTRUSTED to the second Great Royal Wives—Bentanat and Merytamun—are not known. They occupied a place of importance near Pharaoh, before even the death of the queen mother Tuya (around the twenty-second or twenty-third years of his reign). Twelve years afterwards (in the thirty-fourth or thirty-fifth years), they were supplanted by Maathorneferure, with in addition another daughter of Ramses, Nebettawy, another Great Royal Wife, a title she effectively received, her hypogeum being prepared in the Set-Neferu (tomb no. 60). In the kingdom, Bentanat seems to have occupied a place of authority with respect to the king:

Black granite statue
of Ramses II.
Museo Egiziano, Turin.

in her sepulcher at the Set-Neferu (tomb no. 71), she is seen represented on one of the walls making offerings of *maat*, i.e. assuming
the maintenance of balance in the kingdom, and thus contributing
to universal harmony—a royal function. In addition, she presented
Pharaoh with a daughter, represented twice in the same tomb as her
mother, and described as "Daughter of the king, his body." Perhaps
her name, Bentanat ("daughter of the goddess Anat") is once more a
pointer to her mother's Syrian links. In truth, there is no written
evidence to determine the origins either of Isisnofret or of
Nefertari. These latter queens, designated by Seti and probably by
Tuya when the harem of the young co-regent was being composed,
would certainly have been selected with the greatest care among the
most notable blue-blooded heiresses; but, as we have said, no clues
as to their origins survive. It should be observed, however, that more
than six years after the union of Ramses to the Hittite princess,
Pharaoh had Bentanat represented in statue form against one of his
"standard-bearer" colossi at the entrance to his Nubian temple
dedicated to Amun of the Ways (in Wadi es-Sebua), built between
the thirty-eighth and forty-fourth years of the reign. This choice
shows the unquestioned place still occupied by the elder of the Great
Royal Wives at a time when Merytamun, Nebettawy, and
Maathorneferure also remained close.

Ramses and Prince Khaemwaset

O F ALL RAMSES' SONS, Khaemwaset, son of Isisnofret, has
remained the most famous; He was also the most talented. The
elder sons of the first two Great Royal Wives embarked on careers
either in the military or the priesthood. One might familiarly char-
acterize the king's fourth son as "the intellectual" of the family,
researching tirelessly in the sacred archives and much concerned
with the monuments set up by the ancestors. By the time he was
twenty and dedicated to the priesthood of Ptah of Memphis, he is
met with playing an active role at funerals of the sacred bull Apis in
the sixteenth year of Ramses' reign. He reappears in the thirtieth
year, again staging the burial of the new Apis. For Khaemwaset,
with his good grounding in architecture, this presented an opportunity to rethink how the bulls were buried and introduce the innovation of boring tunnels comprising rooms the number of which
had been increased following the deaths of the new hypostases of
Ptah-Sokar-Osiris. His example was followed until the later epoch
for sacred animal cemeteries, in particular at Tuna el-Gebel.

Following pages:
Prone colossus of
Ramses II. Memphis,
palm plantation
of Mit-Rahineh.

Perhaps Khaemwaset was influenced by the projects of Ramses, as the creator of the original and vast underground pantheon facing his own tomb in the Valley of the Kings. Above the sacred necropolis, Khaemwaset also erected a temple reserved for the public cult of Apis and for the ceremonies preceding their entombment.

An archaeologist at heart, and receptive to the splendor of the monuments of the past, Khaemwaset started restoring them in the desert of Sakkara and Giza. Undoubtedly, he bore in mind the initiative taken by his father long ago at his consecration, when he had had the tombs of the first pharaohs in Abydos repaired. He also restored, both in the name of Ramses and his own, the step pyramid of Djeser (Third Dynasty), that of Shepseskaf (Fourth Dynasty), those of Unas (Wenis) and Sahure (Fifth Dynasty), and the solar temple of Neuserre (Fifth Dynasty). An inscription accompanied each repair, specifying the name of the sovereign whose monument had been renovated, as well as mentioning the department organized for the offerings and that of the personnel. Khaemwaset put to work quarrymen assigned to the rebuilding of the damaged parts of the main enclosing limestone wall at the complex of Djeser (Djoser) in Sakkara. Djeser, the first pharaoh of the Old Kingdom, was, at the time of Ramses, rightly considered as "the inaugurator of stone."

Scene of funeral of the bull Apis: the mummy deposited in a naos *is protected by Isis and Nephthys and reposes on a funerary boat drawn on wheels.*

*Funerary complex
of the pyramid of Djeser.
Saqqara.*

The scholars show good sense

I N THE MEANTIME, WHEN THEY noted the damage caused by time
and men in spite of the care lavished on the monuments by
Ramses and the high priest of Ptah, various luminaries and sages
could not resist expatiating on the inanity of these prestigious but
only material testimonies, so manifestly perishable in comparison
with the eternity of the creative mind: "A book is more worthwhile
than a sturdy house. . . ."

Still, the reputation of Khaemwaset has echoed down the centuries, like that of Ramses. The literature of the later period, at the
time Herodotus visited Egypt, continues to emphasize the scholarly
and magical talents of this preferred son of Ramses: the Greek historian reports that he had been informed of an inscription referring to
the prince's work safeguarding the pyramid of Cheops. Wasn't it this
first recorded Egyptologist who, during excavations at Giza, exhumed
the statue of the eldest son of Cheops (Khufu), Prince Kewab, and
exposed it in the temple of Memphis?

High priest of Ptah, and consequently administrator of all the
god's property, his closest assistant was his own eldest son, another
Ramses, whereas his second child, Hori, thereafter became high
priest of Ptah in his turn. Much later, a grandson of the same name
came into the post of northern vizier.

Very close to his father, his function as high priest of Ptah at
Memphis naturally meant that he was involved in proclaiming and
organizing Pharaoh's *sed* festivals: assisted by Vizier Khay for the first
five celebrations (up to the forty-second year of the reign, that is), he
discharged his responsibilities with talent.

From the third to the fourth jubilee

The third jubilee

ONCE MORE PREPARED AND CONDUCTED by Khaemwaset, the third jubilee was as elaborate as its predecessor. For this period of general jubilation, taking place between the thirty-sixth and thirty-seventh years of the reign, foreign princes were once again received at Pi-Ramesse, and then in Memphis.

The new face of Ramses

Pharaoh convened Huy, onetime envoy to the noble daughter of the Hittite and since promoted viceroy of Nubia in the place of Paser, and ordered him to correct all the depictions in the *speos* of Meha showing him performing his devotions before couples of godlike forms: it was now imperative to insert the form of Pharaoh among the divinities. From each sacred group, Huy leveled off one of the figures, re-carving it a little further back. Into the space opened between the two subjects, he would intercalate a representation of his king as rightful heir in the newly constituted triad. As the plaster masking these retouches has since fallen away, in the great court and the hypostyle hall of Meha one can now detect traces of the original compositions.

The assertion of his promotion to a divinity actually formed part of a plan Ramses had long nursed. Since the décor for the Nubian temple of Derr, dedicated to the glory of Re, was still being created, there was no need to modify the reliefs there. Ramses' divine image appears in the guise of a living rebus of his throne name, User-Maat-Re. Human in stature and dominated by the solar disk of Re, he holds in one hand the *user* scepter, and in the other the feather of *maat*. The reliefs on the walls in the southern side rooms of the "treasury" of Meha recalling the precious cult statuettes deposited on the benches carved out of the rock were now complete: the depiction of Ramses, human-faced with a divine horn encircling the ear, or else with a falcon's head, there appears among the gods. There he is called, baldly, *Pa-Netjer*—the god.

Cordial relations with the Khatti

If there was one area in which Ramses managed to shake off the attitude and language of "god on earth," it was in his relations with the Hittite royal family, and the rapport between the two sovereigns continued to improve. Their correspondence demonstrates that Crown Prince Hishmi-Sharruma traveled to Egypt, where he voiced unreserved admiration for the relief decorations on the religious buildings, the monumental hieroglyphics and stone sanctuaries that must surely have influenced the construction and ornamentation of the great Anatolian temple of Yazilikaya, near Hattusha.

It is also certain that contacts arose between the prince and the sons of Ramses. As was his wont, Ramses wanted to go further than simply receiving the crown prince: he desired a visit from Hattusilis himself. A number of propositions to this effect were addressed to his Hittite "brother", but, in spite of Pharaoh's insistence, there was no positive reaction. The relationship with the court at Hattusha fostered links between the two chancelleries, all the more so since frequent requests were addressed to Pharaoh, chiefly concerning Egyptian remedies and doctors who enjoyed an enviable putation beyond the country's borders for several centuries.

Viceroy and builder

Nevertheless, Ramses was keen to give fresh impetus to the construction schedule for Egyptian Nubia—the land of Wawat—drawn up at the foundation of the *speos* of Meha and Ibshek. He was about to replace Huy, his adroit old helpmate, with a thrusting young senior official, Setau, who had been first "ward" then chief scribe to the palace. He placed him at the head of his large southernmost province. From the thirty-eighth year of the reign, this new viceroy exercised his authority on the regions of Wawat, but also of Kush, and more especially saw it as his duty to establish new foundations. He was to work completing Derr (dedicated to Re), as well as undertake the construction of the great Temple of Amun, where the caravans from the huge desert of Libya unloaded. This constituted yet a new altar of rest for the sacred barque, as it floated on the waters of the Flood. After its departure from Meha and Ibshek, the vessel would be received at its station at Derr and then set out, only to halt again in the domain of Amun, today called Wadi es-Sebua. During this new construction, it was of course imperative to place the image of Ramses directly among the depictions of the divine.

The First Prophet of Amun, Bakenkhons

In the thirty-ninth year, following the retirement or death of the brilliant Paser (in the thirty-eight year), Ramses appointed a new high priest of Amun, Bakenkhons, an exceptional religious functionary whose career had unfolded entirely in the service of the temple. Son of the second prophet, Roma, he passed his early childhood under his father's wing before, after a period at the school of the Temple of Mut in Karnak, for twelve years he occupied the post of head of the training stables under Seti I. Then, from seventeen to twenty, he became a simple *wab* ("pure"). From twenty-one to thirty-two, he bore the title of Divine Father. He subsequently accepted the charge of Third Prophet, occupying it for fifteen years. Elevated to Second Prophet until the age of fifty-nine, it was only fitting that he be promoted to the seat of First Prophet of Amun between his sixtieth and eighty-sixth year.

A contemporary of Pharaoh—most likely only a few years younger than his master—it was he who probably conducted a master he had served with unimpeachable fidelity to the House of Eternity. With encouragement from His Majesty, each day more eager to devote his time to pious works, Bakenkhons busied him himself with the priesthood and the architectural enrichment of the temple of temples, Karnak. He managed to surround himself with singularly effective architects and craftsmen, such as the grandson of General Urhiya and the head of security, Hatia, who, *inter alia*, set up "the great flagpoles for banners in the Temple of Amun," and Nakhtdjehuty, Overseer of Carpenters and Head Goldsmith. The silversmiths remain celebrated for the sheets of gold and electrum beaten on to several doors in the sanctuaries and, it would appear, on up to twenty-six portable sacred barques. It can safely be said that, as viceroy of Nubia, Setau left no stone unturned in his search for the country's gold!

Facing page: The great priest of Amun, Bakenkhons. Egyptian Museum, Cairo.

Towards a popular attitude to the divine

In this period of great wealth in the land, Ramses was not solely concerned with enriching the sanctuaries at Karnak. He applied himself still more diligently to developing the cult in accordance with the reforms it had been undergoing for many years, but which war and diplomatic efforts had deferred. He had attempted, with a measure of success, to widen cognizance of the divine. He now wanted to try to give the common people greater access to the house of god, in the same manner as he had introduced the guilds of his craftsmen to writing.

The results had already been felt in the humble prayers addressed by the people, revealing of what has been called "the religion of the poor." As a suitable site for his project he chose the east of Karnak, near the spot where the unique obelisk had been set up, the cynosure of the solar cult in the domain of Amun. In advance of the axis down which the obelisk had been erected, he had a new building constructed containing a monumental statue of himself; through a kind of wide, east-facing window, prayers were to be addressed directly by his subjects to the Pharaoh-god so that he might intercede with his divine peers in the realm of the higher forces.

*The Great Temple
of Amun and the sacred
lake at Karnak.*

Bakenkhons was undeniably worth his salt to his overlord: he had faithfully exercised the priesthood with kindliness, and his talents as a builder and decorator, sometimes also as a judge, had even earned him the right to set up his own statue in the temple. At the height of its glory, the temple of "Ramses-beloved-of-Amun-who-hears-prayers" must have been one of Bakenkhons' most splendid architectural achievements. He left his name affixed to the façade, which was called in his lifetime the "door of Beki," Beki being a diminutive of Bakenkhons.

The period of the fourth jubilee

ON THE EVE OF THE JUBILEE YEAR, in the thirty-ninth year of the reign, the second son of the king, General Ramses, received a title of "heir," the precise import of which is not known. The fortieth year coincided with the announcement of the fourth jubilee throughout the country, proclaimed once more by the high priest of Ptah, Khaemwaset, and Vizier Khay. To the name Ramses-beloved-of-

Amun was henceforth to be added "god, sovereign of Heliopolis."
Egypt had begun to grow accustomed to the spectacular ceremonies
of the *sed* festivals, which were seconded by the traditional feast days
and pilgrimages. For the occasion, the high priest of Osiris ordered
new statues in noble metals in honor of the king in Abydos.

Abundance can lead to excess...

The foreign provinces offered regular tribute, and gold continued to
flood in from Nubia; the country reveled in its wealth, with no longer
any need to levy troops for wars that remained only a distant
prospect. Only the major building works required large-scale labor
requisition, mainly in the periods of flooding. The administration,
too, was notably stable—as long, of course, as the civil servants in
charge of the various departments remained fair and above board...

   This was, for instance, no longer the case in the craftsmen's guild
at Deir el-Medineh, where the departure of Ramose, scribe of the
(royal) tomb, had opened the way to the promotion to his functions of
his adopted son, Kenherkhepeshef. Dishonest practices as old as the
hills soon raised their ugly heads, such as the co-opting of workmen
and artists for personal use. Furthermore, Vizier Khay, preoccupied
with the preparations for the fourth jubilee throughout the country,
had also aroused dissatisfaction, and complaints were lodged about
the late payment of wages. A certain laxness in working practices
starts to appear.

Pyramidion of the royal scribe, Ramose, from Deir el-Medineh. Museo Egiziano, Turin.

A visit from Hattusilis?

The jubilee rites now seemed genuinely necessary to the effective
rejuvenation of His Majesty. Aged sixty-five, Ramses was hit by the
onset of cervical osteoarthritis. His overriding concern was the work
at Karnak, the maintenance of his harmonious temple at Abydos, and
especially of those in Nubia with their crucial message. Above all, he
longed for Hattusilis to visit him in his palace at Pi-Ramesse. The fact
that earlier attempts had proved fruitless did not mean he had let the
idea drop, but now he encountered a fresh difficulty: the health of
the chief of the Khatti. The excuse given for this new postpone-
ment of the voyage was a disease contracted by Hattusilis that
resulted in a painful inflammation of the feet; it does not seem to
have been merely a get-out. Following a premonitory dream of
Queen Pudukhepa's, however, the king was cured, and thanks
were promptly offered to the goddess Ningal, who had answered
the prayer. Thus a letter, in which one learns that the Khatti had left
the city to head for Egypt, seems to imply that the two great signato-
ries of the treaty were finally to meet. The chronicle, however,

remains silent as to whether the uncle and Urhi-Teshub, the repentant nephew, were ever reunited.

This subject apart, exchanges between the two potentates encountered no major stumbling-blocks; on the contrary, relations between the countries warmed still further, since both were anxious to maintain the peace they had forged together. It was necessary to leave tangible trace of Hattusilis's exceptional visit to the "great sun" of Egypt. The idea was aired that Pharaoh be offered another princess to help him regain his youth, something the jubilees alone appeared unable to ensure. To this Hattusilis consented.

Physicians are consulted

As was usual, Hittite demands addressed to Pharaoh frequently concerned his marvelous doctors, whose cures were performed thanks both to their knowledge of botany and elaborate decoctions and because they possessed a thorough-going knowledge of the human body. Some time around the fourth jubilee, there was a surge in the flow of letters between the two courts, from which it transpires that certain vassals of the Hittites were asking for assistance from Egyptian practitioners. When Hattusilis transmitted a request from the princeling Kourounta, "a great lord," to Ramses, the latter replied that he would send him his finest specialist, a man who had already been dispatched abroad many times.

One amusing anecdote, that encapsulates the omniscience credited to Egyptian doctors and exemplifies the caustic and imperious attitude of Ramses, concerns a personal request from Hattusilis about his sister's long-term sterility. Here is Pharaoh's answer: "She's meant to be [only] fifty? . . . Never! She's sixty if she's a day! Nobody can manufacture drugs to make her have children [at that age]! But, naturally, if the god of the sun and the god of storms desire it, I shall send [a good magician] and a good doctor and they will prepare her some drugs to aid procreation. . . ."

Pharaoh's new wedding

At the end of the fortieth year of his reign, Pharaoh prepared to receive a second Hittite princess. Was Maathorneferure, who now resided at Pi-Ramesse, as delighted as she might be to be reunited with her sister? Admittedly, news from her homeland was not in short supply, and she had seen the messengers from the Khatti come to the palace and then the increasing rate of festivities celebrating the visits from her brother and her father. But now was she going to stay in the palace—or was she to repair to the apartments of the great harem of Mi-Ur, or that of Memphis, and cede her place alongside Ramses to her sister, as might be supposed? The question has yet to answered.

On the other hand, the dowry granted by the Khatti appears to have been considerable, all the more so since vassal sovereigns also contributed a great deal to the efforts of Hattusilis and Pudukhepa. This additional testimony to the concord between the two greatest powers of the time must have cause a great stir and further fed a legend that was to echo down the centuries. In Egypt, poets were once again solicited, and several temples shelter steles from which we learn that the dowry treasure was miraculously conveyed without the assistance or protection of men, but by the gods—as was only right for a son of Ptah-Tenen! In spite of an abundant literature, the name of Ramses' second Hittite wife remains unknown. Was she ever promoted to Great Royal Wife? And if so, did she act in "tandem" with one of the recent royal princesses? And was she the Hentmire whose tomb was also prepared in the Set-Neferu? There is a dearth of documentation for this later period of the august sovereign's life.

The death of Hattusilis

In the forty-second year of the reign, carrier pigeons and messengers informed Ramses that the Great One of the Khatti had just passed into the vast and tremendous realm of the god of storms. He was succeeded by Prince Hishmi-Sharruma under the name Tudkhalia IV. It appears certain that good relations between the two countries were maintained, until gradually falling away following the death of Ramses.

The period of the fifth jubilee

For the last time, Prince Khaemwaset, still assisted by Vizier Khay, celebrated the fifth jubilee of his father, who was about to enter his sixty-eighth year. A few months previously, Ramses had had a festival staged for the wedding of his twenty-third son, Samuntu, undoubtedly a scion of a secondary wife, with the young Iryet, daughter of a wealthy Syrian naval captain. His octopus-like family was reaching out its tentacles, in the political as in the religious fields; Pharaoh had every intention of extending horizons.

The completion of the temple of Amun

Still focusing much of his attention on the Nubian foundations, it seemed to Ramses that construction work on the temple of Amun at the terminus of the caravan roads at Wadi es-Sebua was flagging.

In the forty-fourth year of his reign, he announced to Setau, his viceroy, that completion of the *hemispeos* was to be speeded up, and to this end authorized him to levy workmen from neighboring areas, a move that also neutralized the activities of certain Bedouin tribes attracted by the rich pickings to be had from the caravans. Given *carte blanche*, Setau, never one to be overburdened with scruples, ordered Ramose, Commander of the Royal Guard, named "Amun-protects-his-son," to undertake raids on the oases in southern Libya in the land of Irem, probably those of Dunkul and Kurkur, and also to put to work the Tjemehu from Marmaris on finishing the great temple.

The hemispeos *of Gerf Hussein*

Once the complex of Wadi es-Sebua was finished and endowed with an imposing *dromos* between the desert and the river, Setau, in accordance with pressing orders from the king, had arranged for the excavation and erection of the monument in *hemispeos* that had to be dedicated to the grand master of the jubilees, Ptah-Tenen. Like the preceding sanctuary, the new one was to be situated on the same west bank, but more to the north of Kuban and the Wadi Allaki, and was to consist of a frontal structure, with an avenue of sphinxes leading up to it and an open-air courtyard bordered by a peristyle with pillars adorned with Osirid statues. After this, one penetrated into an inner sanctum hewn out of the rock.

Setau does not seem to have been especially demanding as regards the execution of the work, started in the forty-fifth year of the reign and the completion of which was tabled as urgent. The statues and reliefs decorating the two sanctuaries present glaring and regrettable variations in quality, differences due to collaboration between artists from the metropolis and less skilled local craftsmen.

At all events, it was well after being revealed as the son of Ptah that Ramses expressed a wish to dedicate a fourth great pious foundation in Nubia. Each was designed to house the sacred barque after leaving Meha and Ibshek so that it might be gently launched on the waters of the Flood that flowed into Egyptian Nubia (the land of Wawat), and relay the life-giving flood down to To-mery. The sanctuary was also to constitute a provisional home for the sacred vessel. At the rear of the Holy of Holies, a broad niche had been set aside for, not three, but four divine forms seated on a bench. From south to north, there were the statues of Ptah, the head topped by a falcon with outstretched wings, then Ramses next to Ptah-Tenen, and finally Hathor. Ramses was additionally depicted above this niche, in a scene showing him presenting offerings to the sacred barque.

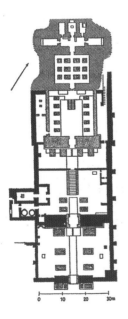

Plan of the temple at Wadi es-Sebua.

In yet another new departure, Ramses is now quoted, on at least seven occasions, as "Ramses-the-god" (*Pa-Netjer*). Moreover, the southern and northern walls of the great court—featuring the six "Osirid" pillars invariably flanked by statues of the king in the costume of the "living" (bare-chested and wearing the royal skirt) in the center—were supplied with eight niches facing each other and containing, dug out of solid sandstone, standing statues of Ramses surrounded by specific divine entities. These include "Ramses-in-the-House-of-Ptah," "Ramses-in-the-House-of-Amun," and "Ramses-in-the-House-of-Re," allusions to the three other cenotaphs intended to receive the barque as it descends to Egypt: Gerf Hussein, Wadi es-Sebua, and Derr.

Avenue of the sphinxes at Wadi es-Sebua. Abu Simbel.

The starting-point was Meha, the place of the sacred barque "Ramses-Flood," which united all that was divine in Ramses-*Pa-Netjer* (the fourth form embodied in Ramses, i.e. Seth). With the return of the Flood marked out by the three sanctuaries, Ramses was inextricably associated with the return of the New Year in his role as "solar child."

One final observation remained to be made concerning this last foundation. Pharaoh had dedicated these temples to the three great divine forms: Re (Derr), Amun (Wadi es-Sebua), and Ptah (Gerf Hussein)—three of the patrons of the great divisions of his army which, in addition, denoted the "tri-unity." It might be wondered whether the imposing *speos* of Meha—where, in the Holy of Holies, Ramses, the "redhead," the Sethian, was flanked by these three divine entities—was not himself one of the visible forms of Seth, patron of the fourth division of the army, in this temple where his kith and kin and his most memorable deeds formed the book of his life.

The sixth jubilee

THE TIME OF THE SIXTH JUBILEE arrived at the end of the forty-fifth year of his reign: the repetition of these festivities had become something of a routine. If Ramses was not getting any

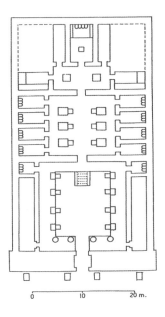

Plan of the temple of Gerf Hussein.

younger and suffered cruelly from the discomforts of age, Khaemwaset, too, was feeling less vigorous, and increasingly delegated the heavy responsibilities of organizing the jubilees to Vizier Khay.

The forty-sixth and forty-seventh years of Ramses' reign

At Thebes, Bakenkhons was busy in court sitting on a tribunal made up of the second and third prophets, the chief of the prophets of Mut, that of Khonsu, four other priests, and the court secretary. The bone of contention was a lawsuit between two heirs, concerning a share of the estate under litigation that might fall to the Temple of Mut. Long gone were the days when Ramses would have delegated one of his family to be kept abreast of such details. Noting his physical decline, Pharaoh, in his sumptuous palace, remained especially anxious to strengthen the roots of his dynasty and the future of his peace efforts.

The 400 year stele

To make the story clearer, Ramses decided to erect a stele dedicated to the form of the divine from which he claimed descent, in the temple of Seth at Pi-Ramesse. The stele, known as the "400 year stele," was discovered at Tanis by Auguste Mariette in 1863 and constitutes an historical element of the utmost importance, despite ambiguities in interpretation. One quickly ascertains that there was absolutely no doubt in Ramses' mind that Seth was indeed his ancestor. The round part of the stele is composed of a central image of Ramses making offerings of wine vessels to Seth; he is wearing the costume of Baal the Asiatic and is holding the Egyptian *was* scepter in one hand, and, in the other, the *ankh*. Behind him, probably, as a statement of his titulary seems to indicate, his father Seti is depicted before he had attained royal rank. The text of the stele implies that Ramses erected it in honor of his ancestors, in order to glorify the name of the "father of his fathers" (Seth) and also that of the late Seti, his bodily father. The follows the date—"year 400." For the first time in the history of Egypt we are faced with the indication of an epoch—prior to this, ever since the First Dynasty, the years had been renumbered from the onset of each new reign.

As Ramses declares: 400 years previously, Seth-nubty, son of Re, the great ancestor, was venerated in these places (corresponding, according to some, to the beginning of the Hyksos occupation). Four centuries afterwards, the inscription on the stele continues, in the fourth summer month, on the fourth day of this reign, there arrives, in this very same place, Seti. Thus, the ancestors of Ramses are all "Sethians," with roots in the region where two high-ranking officials appear, Pa-Ramessu and Seti, before they go on to found the Nineteenth Dynasty, which, like the Fifth, was (in an allusion to the first known theogamy) borne in the bosom of a temple singer of Re. Seth had bequeathed his coppery hair color to his line, the most famous of whom, let there be no doubt, is Ramses. The 400 year stele appears to see Pharaoh in the twilight of his years, explaining exactly what he was and what he wanted to be. Born of Seth, he was intent one last time to reaffirm his origins, the bedrock of his legitimacy, but also, in this hybrid— one might almost say, ecumenical—image of Seth-Baal, to under-line the indisputable identity of these divine forms that he envisaged as a factor for peace amongst nations.

The death of Meryatum

BORN TO NEFERTARI, PRINCE Meryatum, sixteenth son of Ramses, resided at Heliopolis, where he had become high priest. One day in the forty-seventh year of the reign, as his father was nearing his seventy-first year, Meryetamun passed away. Among the innumerable members of the family at the obsequies were his three elder brothers: the crown prince, elder son of Nefertari and Ramses, Sethherkhepeshef, General Ramses, and the high priest of Ptah, Khaemwaset, both sons of Isisnofret.

Curved top of the "400 year stele": Ramses, followed by the first Seti of the family, venerates Seth-Baal. Egyptian Museum, Cairo.

The seventh jubilee

I N THE FORTY-EIGHT YEAR OF his reign, the ceremonies for which Ramses had such high hopes were celebrated once again. His high priest of Osiris and friend, Wennofer, had just consecrated a new statue at Abydos to him.

Two further losses

In the fiftieth year of Ramses' reign, Wennofer gave up the ghost and joined Osiris. His function was immediately transmitted to his son, Hori. The latter would in turn be succeeded by his grandson Yuyu. The palace was now in a permanent state of mourning, as shortly after this the eldest son of Isisnofret, General Ramses, died.

The eighth jubilee

I N THIS WAY, THE ELDEST SONS of the first two Great Royal Wives began to depart from Pharaoh, who, now in his seventy-sixth year, had lost his vigor and was growing weary of the jubilee ceremonies, which he seems to have attended only from afar.

Ramses' final rebus

To conclude the treaty signed with the Khatti, however, Ramses had to continue maintaining harmony between beliefs and cults. In this field, there was still work to be done. He ordered an imposing sculpture group to be carved in gray granite, representing a magnificent monumental falcon with its face reserved in limestone, protecting between its legs the image of a royal child (*mes*), with a finger to the mouth, squatting down and dominated by the solar disk, *ra*, and holding a *su*-plant. This reconstitutes the birth name of Pharaoh: *Ra-mes-su*. Whatever the form of divinity expressed, he is the son of the solar immanence. Thus, dominated by the image of the falcon, in the inscription at the base of the monumental bird one would expect to read the name of Horus. Far from it. The sovereign is loved of Hurun, a divine aspect worshipped primarily in the Semitic regions of Syria-Palestine, but also popular in the land of the Hittite. The Asian colonies of this eastern area of the delta would have been delighted to identify an aspect of Hurun in the powerful Horus.

The death of Sethherkhepeshef

In the fifty-second year of Ramses' reign, inscriptions suggest that, by order of Pharaoh, Prince Khaemwaset, grand priest of Ptah, was

*Horus-Hurun protects
Ramessu, written in a
rebus. The rebus: ra = solar
disk/mes = the royal
child/su = the plant he
holds. Egyptian Museum,
Cairo.*

to be considered as crown prince (but not as co-regent)—a decision that becomes clearer when we learn of the demise of Sethherkhepeshef a little later, in the fifty-third year of the reign.

The ninth jubilee

FESTIVITIES RESTARTED IN THE fifty-fourth year. Prince Merenptah, whose significance was growing daily, delegated Yupa, son of Urhiya, high steward of the temple of Amun and the Ramesseum, to announce the event (1226–1225 BCE). During this period, Pharaoh had the painful duty of being carried to Memphis, to the deathbed of the high priest of Ptah.

Death of Khaemwaset

In the fifty-fifth year of Ramses' reign, Khaemwaset also departed him. For his eightieth birthday, there was little for Ramses to do but weep for a much-loved son who, in his ambition to penetrate the secrets of the divine, had worked so hard with him on the new sanctuaries. Khaemwaset, high priest of Ptah and the world's foremost archaeologist, died after serving the god Ptah-Tenen for forty years. It seems that he insisted on being buried in one of the underground galleries of the Serapeum at Memphis that he had himself brought into being. At all events, in 1853, Auguste Mariette, director general of Egyptian Antiquities at the time, discovered in these buildings vestiges which must have belonged to the funerary appurtenances of the prince: his gold mask and parts of the treasure, including sumptuous gold cloisonné jewelry in the name of Pharaoh, in all probability gifts from his father.

The tenth jubilee

ORGANIZED BY A NEW SOUTHERN vizier, Neferrenpet, the jubilee for the eighty-two year-old Pharaoh took place in the fifty-seventh year of his reign. At the beginning of the sixtieth year, the throne was to all intents and purposes vacant. Prince Merenptah, the last son born to one of the first Great Royal Wives capable of reigning,

Merenptah.
Musée du Louvre, Paris.

was most probably invested with the responsibilities of a regent. It may be supposed that he married his sister Isisnofret II, and also Bentanat II, daughter of his elder sister, Bentanat I.

The eleventh jubilee

Funerary mask of Prince Khaemwaset. Serapeum at Saqqara. Musée du Louvre, Paris.

A ND STILL THE JUBILEES CAME and went. The eleventh was proclaimed in the sixtieth and sixty-first years of Ramses' reign by the Southern vizier and mayor of Thebes, Neferrenpet. Needless to say, Pharaoh, racked by arteriosclerosis, never left the palace. The doctors, among them the priests of Sekhmet who had been victorious over so many ills in Egypt and had been so frequently posted abroad, confessed that the disease was beyond them. Only the marvelous plants from which they made elaborate decoctions could alleviate the pain. To get him to sleep for a few precious moments, these were given to Ramses to drink, often mixed with his favorite beverage, *kyphi*.

The twelfth, thirteenth, and fourteenth jubilees

N ow the rate of the *sed* festivals accelerated, relying still more on their mysterious power to perform one last miracle. Thus, the twelfth jubilee was celebrated during the sixty-first and sixty-second years, the thirteenth in the sixty-third and sixty-fourth, and the fourteenth in the sixty-fifth and sixty-sixth. The sixty-seventh year of Ramses' reign had just started... But then his heart, which had beaten for some ninety-two years, finally stopped, and the Great Guide, the faithful dog-headed Anubis, took his hand. It was at the beginning of the Flood of 1213 BCE.

Amulet representing a "bow" of Isis in the name of Khaemwaset. Musée du Louvre, Paris.

7

THE
LAST MIRACLE
OF RAMSES

New Year's Day, July 1213 BCE

T HE FOURTEENTH JUBILEE OF Pharaoh had been celebrated but, throughout the entire ceremony, since he was now more than ninety, the monarch no longer left his palace of Pi-Ramesse. He had looked on as so many of his children had died, yet he continued to live, to the point that it pained him.

To restore to Pharaoh something of his youth, and with the designation of his thirteenth potential successor to the throne, Prince Merenptah, son of the second Great Royal Wife, Isisnofret, Pharaoh's kith and kin, had opted to step up the rhythm of the regenerating jubilees and have them celebrated every two years. During the last ten years of Ramses' reign, then, the tenth to fourteenth *sed* festivals followed one another in quick succession. In such conditions, it was generally expected, there was no reason why Pharaoh, whose glory had become a legend, might not reach a hundred and ten, an age believed to be the prerogative of the wise. And so the proclamation of the New Year was received with great hope throughout the land. The dry season, *shemu*, was coming to a close, and the arrival of fresh, pure water, the water of the Flood, was awaited with bated breath. As usual, from the very start of May, the vizier had regularly kept the palace informed of the flow patterns of the Nile, and as to when the river receded and reached its lowest ebb. An increase in water was monitored at several points, but especially at Gebel Silsileh. Close to the great steles in the Ramesside chapel arranged in the western cliff, offerings had been thrown in the river to render it propitious to life.

The Flood breaks

T HE EVE OF THE LONG-AWAITED DATE, the Night of Re—New Year's Eve, as it were—had been celebrated warmly. A multitude of small lamps, lit in the doorways in every house and building, answered the twinkling of the stars. And then, on the first day of the first month of the season of *akhet*, a little after July 18, 1213 BCE, the floodwaters arrived in a blazing heat now tempered by the *etesiae*, welcome summer winds which, coming in from the north, ruffled the surface of the river and slowed its seaward descent.

Already the Land of Egypt looked like a sea on which a flotilla of boats, decorated with flowers and streamers, bobbed about to the sound of tambourines and double pipes. New Year's Day had indeed come, and, bedecked in all their finery, all present drew the clear water to drink it or to store it in earthenware jars in which the "lees" would settle; or even send it abroad, as a talisman and

evidence of fecundity. A great deal of "new wine" was drunk! Thus the first day of the first month of the year was noisily hailed: the month of Thoth—that is, of intoxication (*Tekh*).

Scene of rejoicing.
Egyptian Museum, Cairo.

Before dawn, on the temple roof, the priests had taken the divine statuette out of the *naos* and set it up with its face turned to the east, so that the kiss of the rising sun might recharge it with divine energy. The birth of the New Year was proclaimed from terrace to terrace, as soon as the sun was seen exceptionally rising, as it did once a year, in the zone of the sky where the star Sothis (Sirius) was once more visible after its seventy-day eclipse. However, in the greatest secrecy, deep in the palace, the same doctors who, on several occasions, had been sent by Pharaoh to the bedside of Asian princes anxious to benefit from their expertise, had gathered round Ramses, watching on, powerless, as his life ebbed away.

The king is dead . . .

ON THE NINETEENTH DAY of the first month of the season of the Flood, the day after the traditional New Year, the king, deprived of his last flickers of strength and weighed down by the relentless pain that bent his whole body forward, was about to breathe his last. In this period of universal jubilation, it had been thought prudent *in extremis* to hold back the proclamation; but once the news became publicly known, the joyful chants were instantly stifled by cries of grief. The surviving children had flocked to the dying man: those his Great Royal Wives had given him, those of his secondary wives, and all the many grandchildren, led by the thirteenth of his heirs, Merenptah, his designated successor, son of the Great Royal Wife Isisnofret. Most probably the by now venerable Bentanat, his eldest daughter and sister to Merenptah, had arrived a few days earlier from the domain of the

Royal Ladies at Fayum, accompanied by Hentmire, one of the last royal princesses, who had also lately been confirmed as a Great Royal Wife.

Very few of the senior officials of the palace who had hurried to the king's bedside had known the prince in his greener years—save for the former high priest of Amun, Bakenkhons.

Ramses' exceptional longevity was to add further lustre to his resplendent legend. In the Nineteenth Dynasty, one would have to have dug deep in the temple archives, into the bowels of the "Houses of Life," to unearth documents recording a centenary, that of Pepi II of the Sixth Dynasty. On the other hand, Ramses' successors would repeatedly refer to the duration of his reign, one they would have much liked to emulate. Ramses IV for one was to have inscribed on a dedicated stele in Abydos his desire to enjoy "a reign as long as that of King Ramses, the Great God, in his sixty-seven years."

Long live the king!

O NE OF THE MOST GRIEVOUS CONSEQUENCES of the death of any Pharaoh would be to upset the balance of the world. To forestall the worst of the danger, Prince Merenptah, now about fifty and already a veteran of a lengthy regency under his father's wing, was, in accordance with the rule, immediately enthroned, while the investiture of the consecration was postponed until after the long period of mourning and grandiose funeral. By the evening of the king's death, his body had been handed over to the mortuary priests for the seventy days of preparation, so that, transformed into Osiris, the remains of the deceased might begin its posthumous journey in search of eternity. The time of silent mourning was about to start. The strident cries of mourners, and the expressive sighs of men "squatting with their heads on their knees," were replaced by acts of grief-stricken prostration. For their part, Merenptah, the princes, and other dignitaries let their beards grow untrimmed.

Women and children lamenting.

The embalmers

F OR THE INITIAL PURIFICATION, Ramses was at first transported to a lightweight construction known as the "Tent of Purification," probably hard by the temple of Ptah, where, to the accompaniment of rhythmical incantations, his body was sprinkled with revivifying water. Then the priests laid him on a mummification table in the "Pure Place," the *wabet*, where, in the greatest secrecy and under the responsibility of the "Overseer of the

Chest depicting the weighing of the pharaoh's heart. Musée du Louvre, Paris.

Mysteries" representing Anubis, "Lord of the Mummy Wrappings," officiants called *uts* were—after washing down the body with natron diluted in water—to momentarily compromise the integrity of his body and remove the brain and the internal organs. An incision was made into the king's left flank in order to withdraw the organs, which were then embalmed. The heart was reinstated in the thorax, together with the kidneys. It was Pharaoh's heart, as the seat of consciousness, which was to undergo the ordeal of the Day of Judgment, as for all his subjects. As for the viscera, they were to be deposited, mummified, in little gold sarcophagi in the likeness of the deceased. These would in turn be placed in alabaster jars in which each organ was identified with one of the "four sons of Horus": Hapy, Amset, Duamutef, and Qebehsenuf.

Material for embalming: wax figurines of the sons of Horus, British Museum, London.

In keeping with traditional ritual, the lower portions of these containers were placed under the protection of four female entities: Isis, Nephthys, Neith and Selkis, in resonance with the four cardinal points. The complements of the mummy, essential for the king's psychic recomposition, had to accompany him to the tomb, surrounded by the "funerary furniture." Now the mortal remains had to be soaked in a bath of natron to eliminate fat and other putrescible materials, before being cleaned with the best palm-wine. Drained and dried on a bed of fine straw, the body, free of impurities, was then transferred to *Per-nefer* or the "House of Vitality."

There, under the watchful eye of the chief embalmer, the divine chancellor, specialists began the mummification of Ramses by rolling up precious strips of the finest linen. Prior to this, the embalming priests had filled out with little scented linen cushions the vital areas of Ramses' body that had had become flabby when the fat had been removed. The lips had been remodeled and false eyes placed beneath the closed lids. The nose, where the cartilage had

been when the hooks used to extract the brain matter had been inserted, was stuffed with peppercorns, while a priest-lector, holding a papyrus bearing sacred devotions, ceaselessly recited prophylactic formulae. A gold ring firmly fixed in place the heart attached to the left top edge of the thorax, which had been entirely lined with diced wild tobacco leaves glued with sweet-smelling resin.

*Bracelet of Ramses II.
Egyptian Museum,
Cairo.*

Ramses is mummified

IN THEIR WORKSHOPS, GOLDSMITHS were busy making the funerary parure: long necklaces decorated with scarabs, symbols of the dawn of the resurrection, divine barques, guardian goddesses either side of the *udjat* (*wadjet*) eye that stood for restored wholeness, images of a standing Osiris holding the scepters of royalty, pendentives in the shape of temple pylons framing representations of Isis and Nephthys preparing for the animation of the mysterious *djed* pillar—all was ready beside an infinity of amulets, and large figures of winged geniuses cut from plaques of gold that were to be slipped into the swathes of the mummy bands at the exact spot where the organs had been removed. As each amulet was laid down, as each piece of jewelry was edged into its place, a suitable prayer was recited by the ceremonial priests. A belt of gold "woven" with multicolored pearls attached the king's legendary dagger with its handle adorned with two affronted falcon heads to his stomach. Solid-gold cots protected the ends of his hands and feet, and rings had been threaded on all his fingers; a flat ribbon of fine gold encircled his head. It had proved impossible, however, to affix level with his forehead the two protruding animal forms of the primordial goddesses, the vulture and the cobra, which stuck out so far that the heavy, solid-gold funerary mask designed to encase the mummy's head and chest could not be positioned directly onto the shroud. Thus these two insignias had been slipped beneath the wrapping, one against each leg of the mummy. The two royal animals decorating the face of the

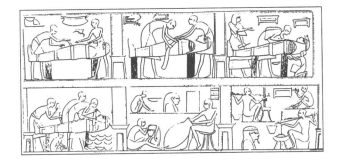

*Making the funeral mask
of a mummy on which
the shroud is laid.*

Pectoral of Ramses II with the vulture and the cobra. Provenance: Memphis Serapeum. Musée du Louvre, Paris.

first and second mummiform sarcophagus were encircled by the small "crown of justification" made of leaves of persea and blue lotus petals. Thus, at the very start of his odyssey to the underworld, Ramses was given all the provisions he would need for his solar legitimacy, confirmed by the ordeal of judgment, to be recognized.

Sarcophagi and vaults

THE MEMBERS OF THE FAMILY were then invited to watch the mummy being placed in the sarcophagi. After the gold funerary mask-cum-breastplate was installed, the mummy was deposited within a first sarcophagus, equally in solid gold, which was then laid into a second in gold-plated wood encrusted with pâte de verre in imitation of turquoise, lapis lazuli, and carnelian. Finally, the successive "packages" were laid in a third external sarcophagus in gilded wood. Ramses was now ready for the journey to the royal necropolis where, since the beginning of the New Kingdom, his predecessors had slept. Straightaway, the new pharaoh, Merenptah, went to Thebes to make sure that the crucial funeral service, organized by the Southern vizier, Neferrenpet, at this time mayor of Thebes, would proceed in accordance with the antique ritual and with all due ostentation.

Ramses leaves his capital

*The female mourners
with the funerary cabin
as it sails towards
the necropolis.*

To the east of the delta, on the shores of the Waters of Re and level with Pi-Ramesse, the great funerary barge was still at the quayside. A platform had been erected to shelter the sarcophagi and the royal corpse. At the head of the floating procession, Merenptah's royal boat sailed against the flow of the river. In his wake, the tug used to haul the funerary vessel was hoisted on two yardarms with a broad horizontal sail adorned with multicolored woven decorations. Assisting the action of the oars, it would help in the struggle against the fierce currents freighted with alluvia of the third month of the Flood (October 1213 BCE). The other barges of the cortège were laden with an immense quantity of funerary furniture for the king, but they also found room for members of the family, senior officials, and for the funerary priests.

Shortly before the river procession departed, residents, peasants, and townsmen alike, alerted by the news it was about to weigh anchor, had massed on the banks: it was sure to be a fascinating spectacle. Of course onlookers marvelled at the lavish manner in which the boats were rigged out, but they could also hear the cries of the women on shore in their weeds, some throwing earth over their heads in grief, answering the traditional refrains of the funeral songs of the boatmen.

A two-day stopover was observed opposite Abydos, the sanctuary of Osiris into whose realm Ramses had just been incorporated. After the preliminary rites of nomination, High Priest Wennofer and his son Hori were taken on board the royal barge so as to escort the deceased to the Valley of the Kings.

Farther to the south, on a line with the immense temple of Amun, the late Ramses and his retinue were greeted by High Priest Bakenkhons and all the clergy surrounding Merenptah. A first stage in the judgment of the departed had probably been performed in the vast court of the temple to monarchy, at the end of which the verdict pronounced by the great and the good among Ramses' contemporaries would decide on the likelihood of his entering the realm of the just. Then the flotilla glided down the immense stretch of water in spate which covered the western plain at Thebes and even lapped the landing-stage at the Ramesseum. Within the jubilee temple, the most archaic funerary rites were recalled and acted out to the beat of chants and dancing, in evocation of the indispensable pilgrimage to the holy cities.

On to the royal necropolis

FINALLY, AT DAWN ON THE PRESCRIBED DAY, the funeral procession left for the tombs of the "ancestors." Since water covered the whole land of Egypt to the fringes of the sands, the river escort sailed close by the long road that starts north of the chain of jubilee temples before plunging into the *gebel*. It then took hours to unload not only the heavy sarcophagus cases, the catafalques, and sled, but also the smaller but equally valuable cargo of canopic jars, as well as all the tomb goods.

Funerary procession Ramses' Tomb, Gurna, Thebes-West.

The procession starts off

T HE SLED BEARING THE CATAFALQUE was pulled by oxen and preceded by clerics pouring milk over the ground. The grieving
parties came in slowly after, in groups following the two shaven-
headed viziers and the "Nine Friends of the Rite," leaning on tall
canes, their skull girt in white mourning bands. Then came bearers
with tall papyrus stems, then numerous disheveled female mourners with their robes covered in the dust they threw on their heads
and loudly giving vent to their despair. At last, the long procession
reached the junction with the beginning of the Valley of the West,
where Amenophis III had had his "House of Eternity" erected. At
this point, the ox team was abandoned, and it was the dignitaries of
the court themselves who bodily hauled the sled with the catafalque
up to the entrance to the necropolis.

The tomb of the king

T HE PLAN OF THE TOMB, MADE GOOD shortly after the coronation,
is more comparable to that of the burial of Amenophis II, which
took the general shape of a square, than to the plan of the shafts,
dug out of the mountain along a virtually single axis, adopted by
Seth I and to which Merenptah was to return. The impressive
alabaster funerary cask had been put in place at the end of the
building work. As they brought in the funerary goods, light from
the torchbearers flitted over the walls of the chamber, revealing
brightly painted scenes in which the sovereign enters into a perpetual dialog with the divine forms of the netherworld. The long
succession of corridors, the walls decorated with evocations of various stages in the advance of the sun—to which the deceased was
assimilated—during the twelve hours of night, led to a first room
with four pillars. This was the "Chariot Room," flanked by two
side-chambers in which officiants would park the king's chariots.

More corridors followed, their walls illustrated with dainty
scenes evoking the mysterious ceremony of the "Opening of the
Eyes and the Mouth" of the mummy, together with statues of the late
monarch. At the end was an ample oblong room called the "Room of
Truth," designed to maintain the balance of the extraordinary prophylactic system that surrounded the remains of the occupant, who
was thenceforth *justified*, awaiting rebirth. After this room, the plan
made a right-angle turn. Through an opening bored through one
of the sides, the "Room of Truth" communicated with the immense
hall of the vault, the "Golden Chamber," the center of the tomb, with
eight pillars and flanked by three groups of annexes. On entering
the "Golden Chamber," a first smaller room on the right was

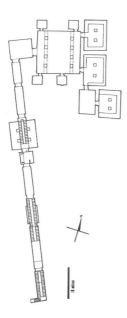

*Plan of the tomb
of Ramses II*

illustrated with the scene from the *Book of the Cow of Heaven*, show-ing a cow, her belly spotted with stars, as an image of the vault of heaven, next to which sails a boat, that of Re, the ageing sun.

In the corresponding myth, men had plotted against the demi-urge. To punish them, he sends down Hathor, transformed into a crazed lioness, with a thirst for human blood. To prevent the destruction of mankind, Re spreads over the earth beer stained red with ocher: this beverage then inebriates Hathor, and order is restored. The demiurge, however, wearies of humanity, and, hav-ing declared: "I had not ordered them to do evil, but their heart dis-obeyed what I told them," he reaches the firmament on the back of his daughter Nut, the spangled cow.

The complex overflowed with extraordinary ritual furniture. In the center of the "Golden Chamber," the bases of the various sar-cophagi were housed in the great alabaster cask, one within the other, while the mummy, standing upright in front of the entrance to the tomb, was to be the object of one final rite—the "Opening of the Mouth and the Eyes," intended to give him back the use of all his senses. This essential task was performed by the king's succes-sor to the throne. Merenptah, dressed in cheetah skin, wearing on his head the *kheperesh* covered probably in ostrich skin, and in san-dals of white hide, would use in turn each of the many utensils placed for the rite next to him on a stool. The final act, made by means of an adze, concluded this "farewell to the dead."

Priest-reader and instruments for "opening the mouth and the eyes," Theban tomb.

Pharaoh's farewell

THE PRIESTS NOW TOOK HOLD OF the mummy, replaced the gold mask over its head and shoulders, then, descending into the gallery once again, replaced it in the sequence of sarcophagi: the lids were positioned on one after another, and the heavy stone top slowly lowered onto the casket. A light tent of translucent linen dotted with gold rosettes and borne up by four gold-plated stakes covered the whole, on to which the four divine canopies were then to be con-structed. Covered with texts and funerary imagery specific to the royal rite, one of the chief roles of the elements placed around the sarcophagi was to reconstitute the chapels essential to the coming existence of the deceased: two figured the archaic vault of the pri-mordial "Mother of the South," Nekhebet, the vulture; a third took the form of the very ancient sanctuary of Wadjet, the cobra, primor-dial "Mother of the North." In this manner, the two entities—recalled, moreover, on all the funerary goods—might accompany the

Following pages:
The Heavenly Cow, accompanied by the god Shu. Tomb of Seti I, Valley of the Kings, Thebes-West.

*Outer casings housing
the sarcophagi of the
king (found in
Tutankhamun's tomb):
a. north vault
b. south vault
c. vault of the Jubilees.*

dear departed in his journey through the underworld. A fourth construction, which was to spread over the other three, took the shape of the great house of the *sed* festival. Its role was to aid in the regeneration and perpetual renewal of the deceased.

Reduced to the most essential officiants, the procession now climbed out of the gallery, avoiding a deep well dug not far from the entrance that alluded to the marshland over which the candidate had to traverse to eternal life, as well as serving to collect run-off from infrequent but devastating downpours.

The funerary banquet

OUTSIDE IN THE VALLEY, A LARGE TENT had been set up for the seats and little tables on which a funerary banquet was to be served for the members of the august assembly. The guests wore necklaces of real flowers all symbolically related to the rites of the afterlife. In the same spirit, they were also presented with sweet-smelling lotus blossoms. To aid in their communion with the deceased, they partook of heady wines which made them drunk as if in divine ecstasy. On leaving the necropolis, the procession circumvented the entrance to a large collective vault (Kher-in-Ahaou) where Ramses had long ago ordered the underground levels of innumerable small rock-cut recesses with the names of his many sons to be carved out.

The successors of the great ruler never enjoyed such a long period of peace as that which Egypt lived through after the treaty with the Hittites in the twenty-first year of Ramses' reign. During the Twentieth Dynasty, Ramses III, however, did manage to protect his kingdom from an invasion still more terrifying than that envisaged by the coalition assembled by Muwatallis. Nevertheless, the country, infiltrated by the creeping influence of Libya and weakened by irregularities in river flow, suffered from the blindness of its central government and considerable shortcomings in administration. It went through a period of poverty and moral laxity that resulted in widespread abuses.

The tomb plundered

CHIEFLY IN THE REGION OF THEBES, where the local authorities were at loggerheads with corrupt officials and hard-pressed to alleviate food shortages, the habit arose of violating and plundering royal tombs. One of the treasure troves to suffer was that of Ramses II, the victim of an attempted "break-in" in the 29th year of the reign of Ramses III, and then of outrageous depredations, even before the rule of Ramses IX. The priceless trappings of his jubilee temple, the Ramesseum, also came under attack. It needed inter-rogation of the most forthright kind to force the perpetrators of the desecration, including a certain Paykamen, to admit to their crimes and denounce their accomplices. To date, not a single tomb in the Valley of the Kings is known to have escaped pillage—save partially for the fortunate exception of Tutankhamun. The royal mummies, almost all deprived of their mortuary finery, were in general roughly unwrapped by plunderers determined to get at the jewelry and gold coverings. To extract the precious unguents, robbers emptied the beautiful alabaster jars, while others even confessed to partaking of the delicious Pharaonic wine! The clergy and the mayor of Thebes then decided to gather the majority of the royal remains together in two of the most magnificent tombs in the Valley of the Kings, that of Seth I and that of Amenophis II, the approaches to which might be policed more easily.

And so it was that the majority of the cruelly mistreated bodies of pharaohs from the Eighteenth to the Twentieth Dynasties, together with the meager remnants of their sumptuous tomb goods, were re-inhumed, without on this occasion great display of pageantry: times had changed! During the reigns of the king-priests of the Twenty-First Dynasty two centuries later, the almost denuded mummies were rewrapped in a paltry shroud of rather coarse linen, while the priceless ornaments had to be replaced by garlands of leaves and flowers.

The "rescuers" re-used the least damaged sarcophagi: the mummy of Ramses II was deposited in one which, in a reasonable state of preservation but divested of its gold overlay, had probably housed the body of his grandfather, Ramses I. The salvage was car-ried out in the sixth year of the "Era of Restoration," the fifteenth day of the third month of the season of *peret* (winter-spring), most probably overseen by High Priest Herihor, during the shadowy reign of Ramses IX, around 1090 BCE. Not long after, intruders again broke into the tomb of Seth I, in the hope of purloining remains of the treasure: the mummy of Ramses was again molested. The high priest of Amun, Pinedjem I, had it repaired yet again in year ten (the date is inscribed on the shroud at chest level). It was perhaps at this juncture that priests placed in the hands of the royal mummiform sarcophagus, plain palm-wood scepters, the flail and the crook of Osiris—humble counterparts of the splendid insignia of long ago

.

A royal hiding-place

IF THE ROCK-CUT TOMB OF SETH I also proved no longer a place of safety, the resting-place of Amenophis II was saved, and was only brought into the light of day in 1898 by Victor Loret. A secret site had to be found to house the sorry relics, a place far away from the royal necropolis, which was too enclosed and isolated. The authorities sought an adequate site deep in one of the great circuses bordering the eastern foothills of the range dominated by the Theban mountain, their choice falling on the hypogeum—most probably previously ransacked—of the obscure Queen Inhapi, in which the mummy of her divinized husband Amenophis I, the patron of the necropolis, had already been entombed. An inscription on the mummiform sarcophagus in which Ramses lay makes clear that the removal was carried out in the tenth year, in the fourth month of the season of *peret*, on the seventeenth day of the reign of Pharaoh Siamon (979–960 BCE). Ramses and his peers were escorted by very senior officials of the clergy, among whom Ankhefenkhonsu, Nespakashuty, and the Chief Sealbearer of the necropolis. The event was made to coincide with the funeral of the high priest of Amun, Pinedjem, buried in the same spot with his own funerary regalia. A fresh official statement was then inscribed on the top of the head of Ramses' sarcophagus proclaiming that the rites were performed by another group of priests, including Djedkhonsuiuefankh, Wennefer, and Efenamun, in the tenth year, in the same fourth month, but on the twentieth day.

This cache had nothing in common with the marvelous underground palaces with walls covered in images of the divine and fantastical illustrations of avatars of the "Son of the Sun" in the transitory universe in which he would undergo his underworld ordeals. The priests first lowered the sarcophagi into a well twelve meters deep and two meters wide. Then the "removal men" entered a corridor. After pushing on some 7.5 meters, they turned at a right angle and ventured down another corridor, sixty meters long, which terminated in five steps, emerging into an oblong, undecorated vault. The difficulty of carrying and dragging such cumbersome sarcophagi through such a place can only be imagined.

Conclusion

So lived Usermaatre-Setepenre, Ramses Meryamun

No Pharaoh left so many texts telling of his achievements and intentions; from no other do we dispose of so many monuments testifying to the motives behind his actions. This might well seem disproportionate in the eyes of modern Westerners—beginning with his astonishing longevity, the duration of his reign, and his innumerable offspring, on whom he lavished such pride and solicitude.

It is true that a number of our contemporaries feel irritated by the mind-numbing reiteration of the titles and praises addressed to a ruler who, to further his aims, believed he had to present himself to his people no longer just as the son of god, as other Pharaohs had done before him, but as the incarnation of the god himself. For much in the writings that the king inspired is patently true. He was undeniably exceptionally gifted; he became his father's co-regent at a very early age: all this is indisputable. From that time, a royal cartouche containing his throne name was bestowed on him.

And was the famous battle of Kadesh actually a defeat? In the immediate future it proved a "stalemate," and only by the skin of his teeth was a catastrophe, brought about by unforgivable recklessness, avoided. Surely it was the uncommon bravery of the king, coupled with a remarkable presence of mind, which, in reacting so quickly to the specter of destruction, saved the day. No! Ramses did not lie and, when it came to illustrating the Bulletin, he was careful *not* to depict the enemy citadel as having been taken. The memory of this battle, which the Hittites seemed to want to put to rest, does appear to have become an enduring obsession with Pharaoh, and his long-term aim was always to retake the positions he had lost in the lands of Canaan and Amurru.

But, faced with an adversary as powerful as the Hittite, who could profit from complicity on the part of city-states ever ready to turn against Pharaoh, it was deemed wiser to deploy more diplomatic weapons. When Pharaoh finally found himself in a position to restart talks with his old adversary and lay the foundations for peace, he seems to have aimed still higher and, to erase forever the painful setback of Kadesh, had, as it were, to make a show of his superiority by marrying the daughter of his erstwhile foe. Although this certainly constituted the climax of his reign, he was lucky to have on the other side of the table a man as respectable, straightforward, and peace-loving as the Hittite.

The wily Ramses discovered how to weave these events into a kind of backdrop in which wonders never ceased. Subterfuge, moreover, had become his lifeblood, a keystone of his character. Thus he had to turn himself into a miracle-worker. His want of royal blood, his unmissable red hair that associated him with the adepts of Seth, the "god of confusion," had pushed him, as it were, to exorcise anything he might regard as an obstacle to his prestige. In this perspective, Ramses appear as the first master of "public relations"—the first in a long line.

Though some mistakenly hold otherwise, his long existence was far from being constantly embroiled in warmongering: at the beginning of his reign there were perhaps fifteen years or so of expeditions and sporadic if dogged battles—out of sixty-seven! The second era partly covers the establishment of peace and the resultant agreements, while the third period of his presence on the throne of Egypt allowed him, thanks to long years of calm in the Middle East and great wealth in the country, to rule for the good of his homeland under exceptional conditions.

An enlightened spirit, surrounded by a group of remarkable senior officials, including an inner circle of Egyptians and eastern Semites mainly of Canaanite, Amorite, and Hurrite origin, Ramses appears as the secret continuator of the Amarnian reforms, both in the arts and in religion. To mask and safeguard this progress, however, he had ostensibly to disavow those who had inspired him, Hatshepsut and Akhenaten, notably by destroying their monuments. Ramses was not only socially aware, but ecumenical too, and he supported the integration of Egyptian and foreign divinities.

Knowing, then, how to turn each event that confronted him to the good of the governance of his country, he could not fail to co-opt the Sothic period during which his family was fortunate enough to come to the throne. He made use of the heliacal rising of the star Sothis and the arrival of the Flood on New Year's Day, presenting these natural phenomena as the consequence of his personal endeavors, shared with the beautiful Nefertari. Master of the Flood, he could thus regulate a calendar on which the rhythm of all life depended.

This unchallenged potentate, this master of wonders, had only one misfortune: to reign too long and watch helplessly as the majority of his elder sons predeceased him. By 1213 BCE, his successor, the thirteenth prince, Merenptah, had already reached a ripe old age when he finally entered into his inheritance. On his demise, Ramses left behind him material ripe for legend. Of all his innumerable descendants, only Khaemwaset, renowned as a scholar and magician, offered fruitful pastures for the writers of the Late Period. The epic of his father, however, has continued to resound down the ages.

2,830 years later

Thanks to the misdeeds of new treasure hunters in the region of Thebes, at the end of the 19th century, the ordeals Ramses had had to pass through in his quest for eternity suddenly made a reappearance in the modern era.

Jars used to embalm Ramses II. Musée du Louvre, Paris.

In 1858, Auguste Mariette, who in Egypt styled himself Mariette Pasha, set up the first department to protect the Pharaonic monuments. Inspectors from the Service of Antiquities soon started supervising the venerable necropolises to prevent them being plundered to feed the hunger of dealers and collectors avid for the choicest tidbits from Egypt's fabulous past. Even before he was succeeded by Maspero, between 1871 and 1874 the area around Thebes continued to provide "antique dealers" with a long line of objects taken from the funerary treasures, as well as papyri dating back to the Twenty-First Dynasty. An investigation undertaken by two of his collaborators, the inspectors H. Brugsch and Ahmed Bey Kamal, concluded on July 6, 1881 with the unmasking of a band of thieves whose members came from a family of Gurna (Thebes-West) and the discovery of the famous "cache of Deir el-Bahri," from which the miscreants would take relics as from an unguarded bank and sell them whenever they felt the urge.

Since, shortly after the discovery of their hiding-place, they surfaced on the antiques market, it was in all probability during this period that plunderers removed from the cache the splendid, deep-blue glazed terracotta vases containing the linen used to mummify Ramses, which the priests had laid next to the king's remains. To date, these represent the only eminent remnants of the great king's funerary property to have come to light. Since 1906 they have been preserved in Louvre.

The emotion on seeing the resting-place of the pharaohs of the New Kingdom, all piled up in a sordid underground chamber at the circus of Deir el-Bahri, must have been indescribable. The often gigantic sarcophagi were extracted in forty-eight hours—but in daylight! Their transfer to Luxor was completed on July 11. Three days later, the ship that Maspero had sent arrived, promptly setting out again with its precious cargo in the direction of Cairo.

Ramses in Cairo

Together with the bodily remains of other dignitaries of his time, Ramses' mummy was deposited at the museum at Boulaq. Henceforth, Ramses was stored near the Nile, prey to extremely harmful damp during the Flood.

The risk to Ramses was exacerbated by a further episode. In spite of the official statements inscribed on the sarcophagi, the khedive of Egypt, H. H. Mohammed Pasha Tewfik, desired to be assured as to the exact identity of the mummies, and chiefly of that of Ramses II himself. At nine a.m. on June 1, 1896, in the presence of seventeen ministers and other high-ranking personages of the kingdom, the process of "stripping" the mummies was set in motion, the whole being orchestrated by Gaston Maspero, assisted by Émile Brugsch and Urbain Bouriant. The fabric used by the priests of the Twenty-First Dynasty to rewrap the mummy were rather coarse, but on the one covering the chest, the name of the king, written by order of Herihor, offered unshakable confirmation of the identity of the corpse.

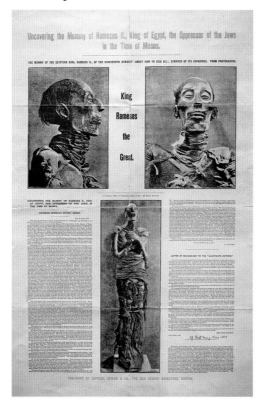

Poster produced when the mummy of Ramses II was unwrapped in 1886.

Henceforth stored in a room on the first floor of the Cairo Museum, the mummies were at least protected from prying eyes, since they were simply off limits to the public. Then, in 1935, they were relegated to the function room in a building erected at the museum entrance, before being transported to the future mausoleum of Saad Zaghlul. They finally made their way back to the Cairo Museum, where they were seen only by the occasional guest of honor.

Ramses in need of care

Another act in the drama unfolded when the authorities at the museum decided once again to exhibit the royal mummies. The climatic conditions, aggravated by the moisture created by the visitors, made their exposure under a glass canopy in leaky showcases that had seen better days particularly hazardous. Requests to X-ray the bodies, the head, and especially the teeth of the Pharaohs came pouring in, and were often granted without the conservation conditions adapted to the undertaking of such scientific investigations being agreed upon. The threat of complete deterioration now hung over the mummies, and I became determined to ascertain the causes of the phenomenon. At that time, the means to do so were not to be had on the spot, so the Egyptian authorities advised me to attend to Ramses in Paris. It was decided to call upon the services of the Dean, L. Balout, administrator at the Musée de l'Homme, and Professor J. Dorst, director of the Natural History Museum in Paris. To make such an operation possible, however, and to transport Pharaoh out of

Christiane Desroches Noblecourt on the arrival of Ramses II in Paris.

Egypt so that "he could consult his doctors in France," it was imperative above all to obtain the agreement of the two presidents, Anwar
al-Sadat and Valéry Giscard d'Estaing, and ensure that the French
government assumed responsibility for our charge.

Finally, entrusted to the capable hands of technical staff from the
Natural History Museum and the Musée de l'Homme, Ramses could
leave the Cairo Museum. Loaded into a Breguet double-decker, a
military aircraft I succeeded in procuring, Ramses performed yet
another miracle in calming the violent winds that might have endan-
gered the cargo.

I took the opportunity of asking the pilot to fly Ramses over the
pyramids. So it was that, 3,190 years after his death, Ramses passed
above the only one of the Seven Wonders of the Ancient World still
standing! At five p.m., Ramses arrived at the airbase at Le Bourget
(Dugny), where he was received in accordance with his rank.

Ramses in Paris

The Republican Guard performed the honors in the presence of the
minister for the universities, Mme Alice Saunier-Seïté, delegated by
the president of the Republic, the head of the president's military
household, and the ambassador of Egypt at that time, H. E. Mr. Hafez
Ismail: the Egyptian government could rest assured that France had
received this ancient and vastly renowned head of state, who had
come to the heart of Paris for treatment, with all due respect and dis-
cretion.

Pharaoh and his 110 carers

Ramses remained a guest of Paris and, more particularly, of the
Musée de l'Homme, where he was assigned a special sterilized
room for some seven months. To detect the agent attacking him
and develop the means to protect and display him safely, Dean
Balout had gathered around him 110 collaborators, all volunteers,
including seventy-three scientific researchers. One learnt that the
king was roughly 5 feet 9 inches (1.75 meters) tall and died aged
about eighty-five. Ramses was leucodermic (i.e. white-skinned)
and of a Mediterranean type close to that of the African Berbers.

At the time of his mummification, his chest cavity had been filled
with many disinfectants: a fine "mince" of *Nicotiana L.* leaves,
nicotine deposits (which begs a question since the plant, it seemed,

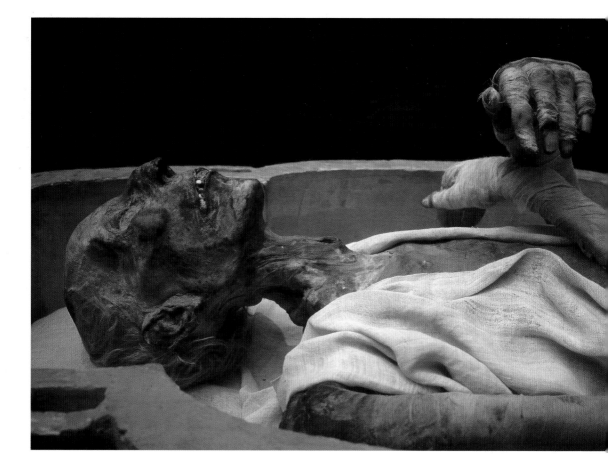

Mummy of Ramses II, profile. Egyptian Museum, Cairo.

was unknown in ancient Egypt), hundreds of thousands of pollen grains of a plant of the chamomile family, as well as sage, buttercup, mixed with gum tragacanth, and lime-tree and plane leaves, and even some wild cotton pollen—all plants from the delta. In his abdominal cavity, fragments of fabrics made with gold and blue threads were detected, while his neck still bore traces of peel from bulbs from a kind of narcissus with an intoxicating fragrance. X-rays of the jaws and a study of the premolars demonstrated that the king suffered significant dental lesions and, in later life, was afflicted with paradontolysis, while the almost blocked blood vessels, visible in the king's head through xerography, proved he had also had galloping ankylosing spondylarthritis for at least the last twenty years of his reign.

In addition, the comparison between the profile of the mummy, presenting a prominent, hooked nose and a protuberant chin, and the side-view of Ramses visible on a photograph from a decoration in the great temple at Abu Simbel, which I had had hung in the room, was striking indeed.

There was another precious piece of information: Ramses had indeed initially been mummified in the north of Egypt, close to his capital of Pi-Ramesse. Data gathered relating to the place where the mummification process must have begun was complemented by observations on the sand grains, of marine as well as desert origin, that remained stuck to the hair. The mummification, then, must have taken place in the delta, at some considerable distance from the Nile (no pollen from aquatic plants was detected) but relatively close to fields, as attested by the heavier cereal pollen.

An unexpected and important revelation

While unbandaging the mummy, Maspero had noted that the white hair had been dyed with henna. Though this fact remains incontrovertible, a very different reason would apparently account for the russet-red color of the hair left at the base of the skull: there, it seems, we were in the presence of natural pigmentation. If the glorious Pharaoh had presented locks of russet-red, the discovery would have been of exceptional interest. In the Egypt of the time, those who had the bad luck to possess such hair, that evoked the color of the sterile sands and the coat of desert animals, were regarded as being in the thrall of the ancient Typhoon, the god Seth. They were pejoratively named "redheaded forms." At the beginning of the Nineteenth Dynasty, however, two pharaohs had received the forename Seti ("he of Seth"). It is as well, then, to bear in mind the manner in which Ramses foregrounds the divinity of Seth, from whom he claims his ancestors to have been descended. He even goes so far as to associate him with the Asiatic Baal; it transpires that Seth appears in the solar myth, not only as the image of the "confusion" necessary for the seasons to follow their course and for the balance of the cosmic forces, but also as an ally of the sun, in whose barque he sails so as to defend it from the Evil one, the dangerous serpent, Apophis. Nevertheless, it was no mean feat to have turned to good account a physical characteristic that could easily have got the better of a less adaptable mind, and to have turned a nefarious disadvantage into something to be held in awe. Far from trying to mask what at other times might have been stigmatized as a handicap, he persuaded the people to see his peculiar red hair as proof positive of his origin in Seth, a divine expression presented as the positive characteristic of his forefathers. Though never declaring so openly in the texts, he so "engineered" matters

Seth, fighting off the serpent Apophis, protects the barque of the sun. Book of the Dead of Cheritwebeshet. Egyptian Museum, Cairo.

that his unusual hair color appeared as a blessing especially bestowed on him by Seth, as a necessary emanation of the sun. A "miracle-worker," Ramses' diplomatic offensive was scarcely less attuned to psychology!

The problem affecting the mummy

When authorization to "treat" Ramses had been obtained from the Egyptian government, a promise was made that no publicity would surround the presence of the king in Paris and that no experiments would be made on the relic: all research and investigations made in our effort to detect the affliction had to be attempted from the outside. The rough fabric placed on it after its arrival in Cairo in its modern sarcophagus was cut into pieces and distributed to various experts, who proceeded to analyze the problem. In the end, it was a chemical engineer of Egyptian origin, an intern at the laboratory of cryptogamy at the Natural History Museum, Mr. J. Mouchacca, who detected, not a microbe, but, "among the sixty or so species testifying to persistent recent fungal contamination, *Daedalea biennis*," a kind of mushroom that had proliferated on Pharaoh's back.

To cure a king

This observation made it possible to plan a course of therapy of irradiation with gamma rays (cobalt 60). Thus, once Ramses' remains had been treated by his "nurses," he was reinstalled in the (restored) sarcophagus in which the priests of the Twenty-First Dynasty had laid him. After being placed in a hermetically sealed display case manufactured specially for the purpose, Ramses was irradiated by engineers of the Commissariat à l'Énergie Atomique, at the Centre d'Études Nucléaires in Saclay. Pharaoh was returned to Cairo as he had come, aboard a French military aircraft, the *Transal*. Once more I escorted him, accompanied by Dean Balout, and the engineer at Tassigny, who had been responsible for the calculations employed to ascertain the correct dose of radiation. As a covering for the great

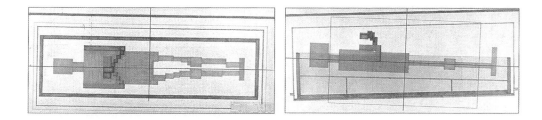

case containing the mummy in his showcase, I had had made by a team of technicians from the Louvre a magnificent lapis-lazuli-blue velvet cloth lined with gold faille and embroidered in golden thread with two heraldic plants of ancient Egypt. Ramses, now cured, returned to his rightful place among his kith and kin in the heart of the old museum. There he awaited transfer to a cenotaph being fitted out to receive him with due dignity, surrounded by almost all the Pharaohs who had reigned in the three dynasties that founded the grandeur of the New Kingdom.

Today, the name of Ramses remains undimmed, a symbol that of itself epitomizes the glory of the pharaohs. And, who knows—in time to come, with the discovery of some yet further "miracle"—perhaps he will have another surprise in store for us.

Diagrams calculating the regular density of irradiation over all points on the body of the mummy.

Index

Proper Names

Aanen, brother of Tiyi 142
Ahmes-Nefertari 100
Amenophis I, 15, 16, 116, 238
Amenophis II, 39, 114, 233, 238
Amenophis III, 15, 39, 48, 106, 142, 232
Amenophis IV-Akhenaton, 13, 89, 93, 94, 104, 114, 142
Ashahebsed, 24

Bakenkhons, 91, 205, 206, 208, 209, 215, 226, 230, 231
Baketmut, daughter of Ramses, 120, 168
Ben-Azen, future Ramessesemperre, 103
Bentanat, daughter then wife of Ramses, 22, 25, 29, 121, 146, 147, 165, 173–175, 179, 198, 199, 221, 226
Bentanat II daughter of Bentanat and Ramses, 222
Benteshima, prince of Ohurru, 55, 85
Brugsch, Émile, 242–243

Didia, 25
Diodorus Siculus, 92

Giscard d'Estaing, Valéry, 245

Hatshepsut, 104, 105, 112, 241
Hatiaÿ, head of security 103, 176, 206
Hattusilis III 142, 144, 145, 146, 154–159, 178, 179, 184, 185–188, 193–197, 205, 210–212
Hekanakht, 147, 167
Hekanefer, 113
Hentmire, daughter of Ramses, 162, 211, 226
Henuttawy, daughter of Ramses 120, 168
Herihor, 237, 243
Herotodus, 203

Hishmi, Crown Prince, 204, 211
Horemheb, 12–14, 16, 17, 21, 35, 104, 156
Hori, son of Khaemwaset, 204
Hori, son of Ptah, 203
Hori, son of Wennofer, 217, 230
Huy, viceroy of Nubia, 204, 205

Imeneminet, 88, 142, 167, 175
Imeneminet, architect, 103
Imenemipet, viceroy of Nubia, 26, 31
Imenemipet, equerry, 48
Imenemwia, son of Ramses, 140
Imenherkhepeshef, son of Ramses, see also Shepseskaf, 84, 88, 120, 121, 129, 143, 148, 159
Imenimipeton 24, 26, 31
Inhapi, wife of Amenophis I, 238
Iuny, viceroy of Nubia, 48, 103, 110, 115, 143
Iryet, wife of Samntu, son of Ramses, 211
Isisnofret, 22, 24, 29, 88, 120, 121, 144, 147, 153, 165, 173–175, 187, 199, 217, 220, 224–225
Isisnofret II, daughter of Isisnofret and Ramses, 120–121, 220

Justinian, 134

Kadashman-Turgu, king of Babylon, 145
Kenherkhepeshef, scribe, 209
Khaemwaset, son of Ramses, 29, 30, 50, 143, 144, 173, 174, 179, 184, 187, 202–204, 211, 212, 215, 217, 218–220, 242

Khay, son of Huy, 168, 176, 179, 186, 203, 208, 209, 211, 212, 215
Khephren, 52
Kourouta, 185, 211

Loret, Victor, 238

Maathorneferure, first Hittite wife of Ramses, 193, 195, 198, 199, 210
Mariette, Auguste, 215, 219, 242
Maspero, Gaston, 242, 243, 247
May, chief builder, 52
Mehemet Ali, 53
Menna, equerry, 77, 84
Merenptah, 102, 132, 143, 173, 218, 219, 224–226, 229, 230, 232, 233, 242
Meryamon, son of Ramses, 139
Meryatum, son of Ramses, 120, 167, 173, 216
Meryre, son of Ramses, 120, 168
Merytamun, daughter of Ramses, 28, 29, 121, 143, 146, 147, 168, 175, 182, 187, 199
Moses, 130, 132–134
Montuherkhepeshef, son of Ramses, 139, 143
Mursilis III, 142, 144–145, 154, 156, 158
Mutemua, wife of Thutmosis IV, 106
Mutnofret, second wife of Ramses, 69
Muwattali, Hittite king, 21, 55–56, 62, 63, 71, 76, 77, 81–85, 140–141, 157, 236

Nakhtdjehuty, Steward of the Carpenters, 206
Nefertari, 22, 29, 42, 48–9, 56, 88, 105, 107, 109–110, 114, 116, 120, 121, 125, 143, 146–149, 157–8, 162–3, 164–165, 168, 173–4, 187,

199, 216
Nefertari II, daughter of Ramses, 121, 168
Narmer, 39
Nebettawy, daughter of Ramses, 121, 198
Nebit, head of the treasury, 53
Nebneteru, 24, 46
Nebwennef, high priest, 46, 48–49, 91, 94, 142
Neferrenpet (Southern vizier) 219, 229

Panehesy, 166–167
Pa-Ramessu, vizier, future Ramses I, 13–14, 21, 216
Pareherwenemef, son of Ramses, 76, 121, 143, 165
Parikhanaoua, Egyptian envoy, 159
Paser, vizier, 24, 26, 29, 48, 59, 88, 91, 95, 144, 158, 167, 175–176
Paser, viceroy of Nubia, 185–186, 188, 204, 205
Paykamen, 237
Pedubaal, 25
Pennesuttawy, 167
Penre, 103
Pinedjem, high priest, 238
Pudukhepa, 154–155, 157–158, 178, 183, 188, 193, 195–196, 209, 211

Raia, father of Tuy, 14
Ramose, commander of the army, 212, 231
Ramose, scribe, 59, 95, 209
Ramses, passim
Ramses as son of Ptah, 211, 214
Ramses as son of Re, 64, 69–70, 216
Ramses, son of Seth, 17
Ramessu, 136, 218
Ramses I, 14–16, 49, 237
Ramses III, 236–237
Ramses IV, 226
Ramses IX, 237
Ramses, General, son of

Ramses, 52, 139, 167, 202, 205, 217

Ramessesempere, 103

Ruia, mother of Tuy, 14

Sadat, Anwar, 245

Salmanasar I, king of Assyria 145, 159

Samuntu, son of Ramses, 211

Samut, scribe, 41

Sennedjem, 26

Setepenre, 44, 64–65, 69, 136, 139, 156, 240

Setau, viceroy of Nubia, 205–206, 212

Sethemwia, son of Ramses, *see also* Imenemwia, 140, 143, 168

Shepseskaf, son of Ramses, *see also* Imenherkhepeshef, 120–121, 129, 135, 143–144, 148, 158–159, 167, 175, 177, 187, 195, 202

Seti, 21–22, 23–24, 26, 29–31, 34–35, 48, 50, 53–54, 57, 59, 90, 104, 106, 115, 132–133, 140, 164–165, 168, 174, 199, 205, 216–217, 232, 247

Seti I, 10, 12–17, 21–24, 26, 29, 31, 233, 237–238, 247

Shapilli, 85

Shattuara II, prince of Mitanni, 145

Siamon, pharaoh, 238

Sitre 14–15, 17

Smenkare, 103

Suppiluliumas, Hittite king, 156

Suty, chief of the treasury, 167

Tassigny, de, 249

Tia, brother-in-law of Ramses, 103

Tiya, wife of Tia, sister of Ramses, 14

Thutmosis I, 105

Thutmosis III, 53, 55, 90, 114–116

Thutmosis IV, 39, 114

Tiyi, wife of Amenophis III, 48, 142

Tudkalia IV, 211

Tutankhamun, 35, 104, 113, 164, 237

Tuya, wife of Seti, mother of Ramses, 14, 26, 28, 46, 56, 88, 104–105, 158, 162, 164, 173, 199
as Mut-Tuya, 46, 88, 108–109, 120–121, 158

Urhi-Teshub, nephew of Hattusilis, 142, 159, 188, 210

Urhiya, General, 25, 88, 103, 206, 218

Wennofer, 94, 142, 175, 217, 230, 238

Yupa, 25, 103

Yuyu, grandson of Wennofer, 217

Zananza, 156

Names of Gods

Amun, 13–15, 17, 22, 26, 29, 40, 41, 44, 45, 46, 48, 49, 50, 52, 54, 57, 65–68, 70–73, 75–77, 89–93, 100–106, 108, 113–115, 120–124, 134–136, 142–143, 159, 165, 167, 175–176, 179, 182, 197, 199, 205–206, 208–209, 211–212, 214–215, 218, 226, 230, 237–238

Amset, 227

Anat, 22, 25, 199

Anuket, 31, 110

Anubis, 173, 221–22, 227

Apis, 144, 199, 202

Apophis, 247–248

Aten, 13, 93–94, 114

Atum, 41, 42, 44, 49, 64, 90

Baal, 65, 66, 68, 134

Duamutef, son of Horus, 227

Dun-auy, 36

Geb, 21, 42

Hapy, 101, 109, 147, 182, 227

Hathor, 15, 46, 114, 116, 122, 125, 148, 173, 176, 179, 182–183, 197–198, 212, 233

Horus, 9, 10, 13, 17, 35, 36, 37, 39, 41, 42, 43, 48, 53, 98, 107, 112, 116, 183, 196, 217, 227–228

Hurun, 217

Iusas, 122

Isis, 31, 32, 37, 56, 107, 125, 148, 202, 221, 227, 228

Khnum, 106, 110, 173

Khonsu, 45, 100, 174, 215

Maat, 15, 26, 31, 40, 41, 42, 44, 46, 173, 176–177, 196, 199, 204

Min, 13, 46, 90–91

Montu, 64–66, 68, 71

Mut, 45, 46, 68, 70, 84, 88, 100, 102, 106–107, 158, 168, 206, 215

Neith, 42, 227

Nekhabit, 40, 233

Nephthys, 227, 228

Ningal, 209

Nut, 233

Onuris, 46

Osiris, 10, 17, 23, 49, 93–95, 101, 104, 142, 147, 160, 179, 183, 199, 209, 217, 226, 228, 230, 238

Ptah, 39, 49, 52, 57, 70, 76, 80, 83, 89–90, 102, 111–112, 115, 124, 136, 144, 173–174, 184, 186, 188, 193, 196–197, 199, 202–203, 209, 211, 213–215, 217–220, 226

Re, 13, 16, 21, 29, 36, 41, 51, 56, 57, 64–65, 68–70, 75–77, 80, 89–90, 92, 94, 100, 105, 114–122, 124, 136, 149, 157, 162, 179, 204–205, 214, 216, 224, 230, 233

Satet, 110

Sekhmet, 52, 188, 197, 221

Selkis, 227

Seth, 12–13, 17, 36, 39, 51, 57, 66, 70, 76, 83, 90, 116, 154, 157–159, 196, 214–217, 241, 247–248

Sokar, 183–184, 199, 202

Sothis (Sirius), 100, 109, 120, 125, 148–149, 179, 225, 241

Sutekh (Seth), 66, 68, 70

Ta-Uret, the Great, 148

Teshub, 142, 159, 210

Thoth, 36, 39, 41, 44, 100, 106, 122, 153, 225

Wadjet, 40

Select Bibliography

This bibliography is uniquely concerned with general works and functions independently of the articles, scientific research, and excavation reports that have appeared in diverse reviews and specialized Egyptology collections.

Desroches Noblecourt, Christiane. *Save the Treasures of Nubia*. Paris: Unesco, 1960.

———. *Egyptian Wall Paintings from Tombs and Temples*. New York: New American Library of World Literature, 1962.

———. *Tutankhamun: Life and Death of a Pharaoh*. New York: New York Graphic Society, 1963.

———. *Paris Post-mortem on Tutankhamun*. London: Hansom, 1967.

———. *Treasures of the Pharaohs: The Early Period, The New Kingdom, the Late Period*. Geneva: Skira, 1968.

———. *The Great Pharaoh Ramses II and His Time: An Exhibition of Antiquities from the Egyptian Museum*, Cairo: Palais de la Civilisation, Montréal, June 1– September 29, 1985. Montréal: Ville de Montréal, 1985.

———. *Gifts from the Pharaohs: How Egyptian Civilization Shaped the Modern World*. Paris: Flammarion, 2007.

Desroches Noblecourt, Christiane and F.L. Kenett. *Ancient Egypt: The New Kingdom and the Amarna Period*. Greenwich, CT: New York Graphic Society, 1960.

Desroches Noblecourt, Christiane and Sir Herbert Read. *Ancient Egypt (The Acanthus History of Sculpture)*. New York: New York Graphic Society, 1960.

Desroches Noblecourt, Christiane and Georg Gerster. *The World Saves Abu Simel*. Berlin: Verlag A.F. Koska, 1968.